THE PATTERN OF PRAYER

The Sangster Library of Inspiration

THE PATTERN of PRAYER

W. E. Sangster & Leslie Davison

FRANCIS ASBURY PRESS
of Zondervan Publishing House

Grand Rapids, Michigan

THE PATTERN OF PRAYER
Copyright © 1962 by the Epworth Press
Copyright © 1988 by The Zondervan Corporation

This edition edited for North American readers and published by arrangement with the Epworth Press, London, England.

FRANCIS ASBURY PRESS is an imprint of Zondervan Publishing House, 1415 Lake Drive S.E., Grand Rapids, Michigan 49506.

Library of Congress Cataloging in Publication Data

Sangster, W. E. (William Edwin), 1900–1960.
   The pattern of prayer.

   Reprint. Originally published: London : Epworth Press, 1962.
      1. Prayer. I. Davison, Leslie. II. Title.
BV215.S24   1988   248.3'2   88-19313
ISBN 0-310-51401-0

All Scripture quotations, unless otherwise noted, are taken from the King James Version of the Bible.

Printed in the United States of America

88 89 90 91 92 93 / EP / 10 9 8 7 6 5 4 3 2 1

Contents

Publisher's Foreword

The Pattern of Prayer will become a treasure to many people. They will cherish it for the enlightenment it brings to the subject of prayer, and because it enables them to know the truth of our Lord's "ask, and ye shall receive, that your joy may be full."

The book contains some of Dr. Sangster's final and most mature writings. This beloved Christian leader dwelt much in the realm of prayer, and what he says on this vital subject was born of experience. During the last two years of his life his main concern was to develop the Prayer Cell (or Prayer Life) Movement, begun eight years earlier by the Methodist Home Mission Department, by fostering the formation of prayer cells (small groups) and teaching their members the art of prayer through *The Prayer-cell Messenger*, a quarterly pamphlet. This ministry was continued by Leslie Davison, and this book is a selection of the writings of both men.

In some respects the Prayer Cell Movement in Great Britain has been a forerunner to the development of small groups on the North American continent. It is this phenomenon that makes Dr. Sangster's counsel regarding prayer groups so timely to contemporary readers and so relevant to the needs of Christians today.

"If ye shall ask any thing in my name . . ."

For the Spirit of Believing Prayer

Heavenly Father, who has said that all things are possible to believing prayer, pour into our spirits such complete faith that what we ask in Your name shall be given to us.

Grant us such a passion for prayer that nothing will prevent our pleading the desires that You Yourself have put in our hearts.

We are sure that if we could pray this way, every other precious thing would come with it.

Give it to us, for our Savior's sake. Amen.

For Revival

Spirit of the living God, we are sad to see our dear land drifting from You. Our churches are often neglected; our prisons are overcrowded.

Many of our young people are turning to crime, and multitudes of men and women in middle age can find no meaning in life at all. Even where we have done everything we know, we have not stopped the drift.

In self-despair we turn to You.

Come upon us in power, as You came upon the apostles at Pentecost.

Come upon us in power, as You came upon the founding fathers of the church.

We need love, joy, wisdom, fire—and all of them are blessed fruits of Your indwelling.

Spirit of the living God, fall afresh on us, for Jesus' sake. Amen.

Chapter 1

The Basic Need

When God intends great mercy for His people,
He first of all sets them a-praying.
                    —Matthew Henry

Only God can know the amount and the quality of prayer offered in this world, but it seems sadly certain that there is less prayer offered than there was some years ago. The size of congregations in Western countries is generally smaller, which reduces the amount of corporate prayer, and many Westerners now claim to be agnostic, which reduces the amount of private prayer as well. An agnostic may still hope that there "might be something in religion," but he doesn't go on praying.

Others may attend church more or less regularly and even hold some office there, but their lives are almost indistinguishable in any other respect from the non-churchgoing multitudes around them.

In some churches prayer is still recognized as man's highest activity. It is intelligently studied and devoutly practiced; it is ordered, disciplined, and judged to be the first business of every day. Yet it must be admitted that those are the unusual places.

But this is not the first time the tide of spiritual power has ebbed. The Home Mission Department, for instance, which is less than half as old as Methodism, came into being when the initial revival was spent and the Conference felt that the whole church needed to be called again to her "first works." It was an effort to recover spiritual energy and to work with other Christians to bring a nation back to God.

The conviction grew upon us that prayer was our basic need, that the things we wanted could only come this way, that programs were useless without prayer. We also believed that the number of prayer meetings was only important if they were of the right kind, and the task was to teach prayer as well as to multiply it.

Why We Need Prayer Groups

Do you think we exaggerate the importance of the right kind of prayer? It isn't possible! Think of the things we most need, and notice how prayer is basic to them all.

We need revival. Prayer is the way. We are quite sure that many things thought to be necessary to revival are not necessary. The 1859 revival had no outstanding leaders at all! But like all the others, it had the great prelude of prayer.

We need assurance. Many people, even Christians, are groping. The number of agnostics and people indifferent to religion increases. How can we be sure of our faith? Prayer is the way.

We need warmer relationships between the denominations. Holding dialogue and fashioning a formula have a part to play, no doubt, but the love that makes us cling to one another is born in corporate prayer.

Everything in the life of the Christian comes down ultimately to secret communion with God—his own consistent quality of living, his deep unshakable assurance, his power to help others, his courage and trust.

There is particular need for people to make sure this divine communion is constant and deep. Nothing would do us more good than that for Christians to check themselves again on these central things and make sure that they really are living "at the secret source of every precious thing."

But something else is urgently needed too. We need to recover again the power of corporate prayer. Something is added to prayer offered in fellowship that is not given in the same degree of the same prayers offered by the same people in separateness. "Where two or three are gathered together in my name . . ." (Matt. 18:20). Through two hundred years of Methodism, men powerful in winning souls have ascribed their success to the fact that the prayer meeting was the central meeting of the week—honored by all, undertaken with businesslike thoroughness, devoid of haphazard railing to heaven, but preceded by thought and conversation concerning the right "objectives" of the praying, being a pleading in the power of the Holy Spirit for the things God Himself desired.

This is our great need: the recovery of range and depth and listening and love in prayer. When we join together in a prayer cell, we are sharing in a vast volume of prayer and are helping to open the impoverishments and perplexities of earth to all the resources of heaven.

Nothing we do is more important than this. The people who brush prayer aside on the ground that "after all, the important thing in the end is what you do" forget that many of the things we do would be different if we prayed first for God's plan, rather than asked for His blessing on ours.

Our prayer is God's opportunity to shape us, our home, and our work, and even our neighborhood, our country, and the world. Ordinary people often wonder what they can do about international problems, about nuclear weapons and world tensions, about incurable disease and the hungry multitudes of the Third World. They are tempted to sink into apathy because of their own helplessness. But God isn't helpless. We have opinions; He has a plan. Prayer opens earth to heaven. It is the way to learn God's plan in situations small and large.

Let us make private prayer the priority of every day and share fully in the life of a prayer cell also. No day is ill-spent in which we have really prayed.

Learning About Prayer

Many people have very immature ideas on prayer. They are often quite perplexed about its inner nature and speak frankly of their disappointment in the results. Yet they are eager to learn. We believe that this book, as small as it is, can teach something very important about prayer. All real instruction on the subject comes, of course, from God, but we believe He will graciously use this book as a medium of His will. We want to encourage Christians in the intelligent understanding of prayer and a loving and wise practice of it.

We want to help people at all stages in the school of prayer—those just beginning, those with things to unlearn, those who are well past the elementary level. We want to be as practical as possible.

The chief purpose of prayer is to meet with God and to have fellowship with Him. Many adult Christians have not advanced beyond the point of childhood petitions in which prayer, taught at Mother's knee, consists of a short list of wants and intercessions for loved ones. While "God bless Mommy and Daddy" is a lovely prayer for a child of five, it has little in it to feed the soul of a person of forty-five. Prayer that contains little more than a list of requests reflects small credit on either God or us. It is a paltry and crudely acquisitive spirit that clamors for gifts and never pauses to think of the Giver.

Although God hears and answers every cry for help, He reveals Himself only to those who truly seek Him. The sobering fact is that many of us want His help to get us out of trouble and affliction, we want His gifts to satisfy our desire for success and happiness, but we do not want *Him.* We are afraid of Him and afraid of what His coming might mean to us.

A girl with a keen mind once put it frankly in her cautious question to me: "How much will I have to give up if I become a Christian?" The coming of God into her life suggested restriction and limitation to her. She knew some Christians who did not drink or gamble or smoke or dance or go to movies. Their negative, joyless piety did not attract her. There were things in Christianity that appealed to her, but the price seemed high.

But even if she had seen smiling, triumphant Christians bubbling over with the joy of God, she would have had to recognize that the price was still high. Those who seek God for Himself and not for His gifts alone must give themselves without reserve, placing their whole being at God's disposal in daily surrender to His will. When we are ready to give all, God gives all; and how much is the all of God!

Therefore, basic to all our needs is the need of prayer. Our failure to recover the vitality and centrality of the prayer meeting is both the expression and the cause of our ebbing life. The words of Charles Wesley speak to God for us.

> Come in Thy pleading Spirit down
> To us who for Thy coming stay;
> Of all Thy gifts we ask but one,
> We ask the constant power to pray:
> Indulge us, Lord, in this request;
> Thou canst not then deny the rest.

Chapter 2

The Art and Craft of Prayer

There is no way to learn to pray but by praying.
—Samuel Chadwick

Can there be an art to prayer? Is it really a craft that demands a long apprenticeship?

Is there not something artificial in the very suggestion? Surely prayer is just talking naturally to God as simply and as easily as children chat with their father.

Of course prayer *is* talking naturally to God, our Heavenly Father. But it is neither as simple nor as easy for us to talk to God as for a child to speak to an earthly father. The earthly physical father can be seen; the embrace of his strong arms can be felt. He answers back and asks questions.

It is a dangerous oversimplification to pretend that talking to God is like that. For one thing, we don't see Him. There are many times when we don't feel Him and when it is difficult to imagine that there is anyone there at all. Often the conversation seems all one-sided. We talk, but nobody seems to hear.

Praying should be as spontaneous, trustful, and satisfying as a child's conversation with a loving parent. But it is one of the most difficult things in the world for adults to put themselves in the place of little children. To do that we must first be born again and grow in the new life of Christ through the Spirit into a state of childlike simplicity and trustful love. Childlike, praying love is the end product of the life of prayer, not the beginning.

Becoming Masters of Prayer

We become masters of prayer as we become masters of anything else—by discipline, patience, perseverance, the careful correction of mistakes, the study of great examples, and the constant effort to improve.

Almost anyone can tap out a simple tune with one finger on a piano, but to be a great composer or a great pianist one must devote all of life to music. Similarly, if prayer is ever to become more than a cry for help, or the first stammering outpourings of the newborn soul, it must be studied and practiced, not just when we feel like it, but regularly year after year. Only in this way will the soul develop wings and learn how to soar.

Some people dislike this talk of prayer techniques because it sounds mechanical to them and "scientific" in the wrong way. They fear that prayer will be made too much like a medicine—quite useless unless the prescription is exact.

We can sympathize with that point of view. God helping us, we shall never become so technical that the simplest member of the congregation can't be in the family too. Yet the School of Prayer has advanced departments as well as a kindergarten, and we want to help people wherever they are. There must be some talk of methods and techniques.

Nor does the advanced School of Prayer belong to the so-called intellectuals. Many "intellectuals" are not in the School of Prayer at all, and some who are humbly admit that they are in the babies' class. Prayer is not chiefly a philosophical occupation. Apprehending the spiritual world and bringing back its treasures is much closer to appreciating beauty in nature or in music than it is to making logical distinctions. It is another way of knowing. Some of the people wisest in prayer would be judged "simple" by academic standards. But Jesus would approve them. They have the simplicity He commended when He said, "Except ye . . . become as little children, ye shall not enter into the kingdom of heaven" (Matt. 18:3).

Even those who most dislike talk of "technique" in prayer will allow that some things about common prayer are wrong. Prayer isn't so holy an occupation that you can't make awful mistakes about it. Indeed, it is because prayer is so important and potent that the mistakes can be shocking and costly. When we talk of "techniques," we are only wanting to guide the unwary from these errors and to deepen their effectiveness in life's highest occupation.

How much prayer is purely selfish! "Give me . . . give me . . ." This is only egotism on its knees. People aren't better for this kind of praying. If they are better for thinking of God, they are worse for being tightly wrapped up in themselves. Only an archangel could strike the balance between the gain and loss of this kind of praying. So if there is a "technique" to guard us from selfishness in praying, we want it.

Or think of the mistakes people have made for years over prayer and temptation. Some fiercely tempted people have carried their temptations into their prayers, have lingered in thought on the very things they should have banished, and have held pictures in their imagination that were deadly to Him—and not less deadly because they were on their knees. They did not know that one overcomes temptation by dwelling on its opposite and by beholding Jesus, the supreme master of temptation, in the center of their thoughts.

Some people are always bored with their praying. Even the best Christians are cold occasionally and have to push themselves to pray, but fancy being always bored! It must bore God! Is there a technique to overcome boredom?

Not all people who are serious in praying for others in need realize that intercession offered merely as a duty cannot do the work. It is love that gives prayer wings. It is love that annihilates distance. It is love that pierces to the heart of a person's need and becomes the agent of divine help and healing—spiritual, mental, and physical. But how can we charge our prayer with love?

Hearing the Voice of God

I received a letter from a man of seventy-three who said, "I have tried for years to hear the voice of God. I have never heard it. Is it all illusion?" He did not know how to listen. He seemed to expect a human voice. To quote the poet and say to him, "God speaks in silences," won't help him; it sounds silly. What is the answer?

How does a mortal man listen in prayer to the living God? The prophets often said, "Thus saith the Lord." They claimed to have received special messages from God. How did they receive them? How did they distinguish these messages from thoughts of their own? Heroes of the faith in times past often claimed that God spoke to them—sometimes in quite precise terms. People of our own acquaintance use similar expressions. Maybe we do ourselves. When we make these claims in the hearing of unbelievers or nominal Christians, we cause more perplexity than we know. *What does he mean?* they wonder. *How does God speak to him?*

Let us attempt to dispel that confusion. Clearly the voice is within our minds. It is not audible in the sense that a tape recorder could pick up the message. We hear it, but others in the room wouldn't hear it at the same time unless (in some wonderful listening session of the prayer group) they also heard it in their minds. At times the voice is so loud in the mind that we could almost think it was outside us or, as Isaiah says, "behind" us (Isa. 30:21). But, pinned down to exact speech and honest experience, we should concede at once that it is in the mind.

There begins the difficulty. Many voices sound within our minds. People who have never practiced listening in the silence are astonished, when they begin, at the pandemonium of voices inside. At times it sounds like Babel. Fear, hope, memory, and ambition all find voice inside us and sometimes they even talk together. The high skill of this interior listening is to learn how to distinguish the voice of God from all the other voices whispering or shouting within. It isn't simple. One must be prepared for patience and practice, and resolve never to use the words "God said to me . . ." or "I was guided . . ." (or any similar expression) without great care and reserve.

Imagine a wireless operator listening on his first voyage across the wide Atlantic. What a riot of sound assails his ears as he moves the knobs on his instruments! Any idea of the "silent air and ocean" must seem laughably ludicrous to him now. How intently he must listen! All his brain tunes in to his ears. Suddenly he gets it! It is not as loud as other calls, but it is his signal: they are calling his ship. On that pinpoint of sound, in all the babble of noises, he focuses the whole concentration of his listening and, as he concentrates, it seems to get louder, clearer . . . his pencil moves . . . the message has been received. The ship's whole course may be altered by that word.

That is a simple picture of the disciplined Christian listening to God. If an unbeliever says flatly, "I don't believe that God (if there is a God) speaks to men and women," that finishes the discussion for him. He has shut his mind on the issue. He won't even experiment and try this listening.

But this faith in God's speaking is basic to the Christian. God is there. He is like Jesus. He is great enough to manage the whole universe and still take a Father's care of each of His children. "When man listens, God speaks."

But it isn't any good for Christians to say they believe in this if they never practice it and, therefore, never experience it. Indeed, that is how a vague hypocrisy creeps into religion and that awful sense of unreality that can plague even a sincere church member. It is personal experience of God, heaped up over the years and firmly based on the Christian revelation, that holds us in the times of life's tempest and makes us unshakably sure.

The question is more central than we may have supposed. The way to learn to listen is to listen—and not to be surprised if interpretation takes a little time.

The nearest word I can find to describe the distinctive voice of God in the babble of sounds within is the word *authority.* The voice has a commanding note. It has a quality of being above question and brings a warm assurance with it.

And therein lies another danger. The apostle Paul says that we have a battle with satanic powers in high places and this may be the reason why this authority is sometimes counterfeited in our mind. People are occasionally misled by a sense of authority within. Anyone who has been involved with the mentally ill at any level is acquainted with people who heard "authoritative voices" telling them to do things that are commonly judged to be wrong.

That is why, whenever guidance appears to run counter to the counsel of the church, one should submit that guidance to a wise prayer-partner or to the collective and unhurried judgment of a prayer cell. Now and then in the long history of the church, men and women may have been led of God to do things which the orthodox of their age did not approve, but which the Christian conscience of later ages has recognized to be of God. Joan of Arc, Savonarola, John Wesley, and William Booth come to mind as examples.

But these instances, thank God, are rare. The mass of men and women need God's guidance directly and by confirmation of the fellowship of devout believers. Most guidance never raises any questions of this kind. When people complain that men are sometimes misled by what they think is God's guidance, it is still pertinent to reply that the number of those so misled is microscopic compared with the number who have missed their way by taking no thought of God's guidance at all.

How do God's messages come? Often they come in the language of Scripture. God selects a text or passage we have known for years and makes it radiate with a new light. It is as though He says, "This is the relevant word for you now!" Sometimes it is a couplet from the hymnal or a chapter in a modern book of devotion or a phrase from a praying friend. But we know it by the different, shining, commanding quality. It is as though God says, "This is it."

Sometimes God borrows our own tongues and talks to us. How wonderful those secret conversations of the soul can be! I could relate many personal experiences here. The greatest spiritual hours of my life have been in these conversations. You raise a question with God and go on talking of your perplexity, and He seems to take over, asking you questions and elucidating answers that were sometimes inside you already and that sometimes come direct from Him. You get to the point where you hardly know who is asking and who is answering; but it doesn't matter. The blessed session leaves you lost in wonder, love, and praise. You can go a long time on the memory of one such exalted hour. Should the time come in which He seems for a while not to answer, you can say in complete trust, "I have heard God speak. I can bear His silence. He will speak again when He is ready."

"Just Pay Attention"

Some of our friends, however, will still say, "We have listened, but we do not hear." Let me see if I can help those people; and if this chapter becomes somewhat autobiographical, you must forgive me.

I wasn't born with an ear for music. It wasn't true, but my brothers used to say that I only knew it was the national anthem because everybody stood up! When it was time for singing lessons at school, they sent me home early.

In my early teens I applied to join the school choir. Actually, I didn't care a thing about the choir, but I greatly admired the music director. If I were in the choir, I would be able to spend more time with him.

The director gave me an audition and seemed a little pained at the end. Finally he said in his crisp way, "Yes, you may join the choir. I will make you secretary." I learned shortly that the secretary didn't have to sing! I was still a boy when I sadly concluded that music was a "closed shop" to me.

It was my committal to Christ that really made me want to sing. Charles Wesley's hymns became a passion. He said so perfectly some things I knew—and more I wanted to know. I still couldn't sing, but I began to "make a joyful noise unto the Lord."

And then I got married, and music meant a good deal to my wife. She wanted it to mean something to me. Too wise to thrust it on me, she would say, "Listen to this, dear. Do you like it?" Often I answered her with a mild grimace, but she never gave up the hope that we could share this happiness together.

The day came when I bought her a hi-fi/radio set. It wasn't "six for her and half-a-dozen for me." I still had only the mildest interest in music myself, but maybe that was how I delivered myself into her hands.

She would get me by the fire for the last hour of the day

and say, "I will play it softly, dear, but if you hear it in the background many times, it will make a path in your brain, and someday you'll say, 'Oh! I like that!'" I loved her for her intentions, but I inwardly hoped it would be very soft, and I just sat reading my book and never really heard it all. Time went by. I think my wife began to despair. "You'll never love it until you really listen," she said one day, and she seemed so sad about it that I replied at once, "Of course I'll listen if it means that much to you." The night came when I put my books away and really listened.

I must be honest: I couldn't get anything out of it. It didn't sound a bit like a Methodist hymn! *I must take this up*, I thought. *What a medley! I don't even know what bit to listen to.*

I went to the library and got some books. Laboriously I started to learn the different instruments. I began to distinguish woodwind and brass, and this and that . . . and then I began to listen (almost with my sleeves rolled up!).

"What's that instrument?" I would exclaim in the midst of some moving passage. "And that?" I listened and analyzed and exclaimed, and I fear I spoiled it for my wife as well. Nor was I any nearer to enjoying it or getting anything from it.

In the end, almost despairing again, my wife said, "Look! Give up analyzing and trying to understand it. Just pay attention to it. Put your mind in your ears and only listen." And—do you know?—she was right. I did just what she said. I listened . . . and listened . . . and listened.

Not much came at first. There were many hours that seemed to bear no return—valuable, necessary hours, as I came to believe later, but nothing obvious at the time. Yet the day came when a new world opened to me, and if I were missing from the family circle when in the house (yet not in the study), they would say to one another with a smile, "He has sneaked off for a bit of music. Listen! Yes, he's in the lounge."

The story has a purpose. Listening to God can require many hours without any obvious return—especially if you listen analytically. Just pay attention. Don't break up everything you hear by a questionnaire: "Was that my subconsciousness? Was it wish or fear? Is that an echo of my talk last night . . . or an overtone of the book I'm reading . . . or a recollection of the television drama?"

Just pay attention. The voices will sort themselves out. God will get through. The fruit of long listening may not come at this time, but quite clearly later, and it will bear its own divine impress and authority. Confirmatory signs will occur. "God," as one godly Scotsman said, "will give His whole mind to your need, as though He had no other soul to save and sanctify but you." The day will come when the most militant and cogent unbeliever will be unable to shake your certainty. You know God speaks. You have heard Him for yourself.

Don't assume that this experience will make it possible for you to "prove" religion to your unbelieving friends. You cannot "prove" the rapture of music to the tone deaf; you can only testify to it.

If, when you speak to a skeptic of all that Christ says to you, he just smiles in a pitying way and murmurs something about your "imagination," don't be disappointed. Religious experience, like the appreciation of music, can't be "proved" either by logic or in a laboratory. One man can't give it to another; he can only explain how he came by it himself.

If, however, your skeptical friend goes on to suggest that our mental hospitals are full of people who think they hear voices, remember the last great concert you attended. Was it in Carnegie Hall, the Lincoln Center, your local auditorium? Were there thousands of other people there, sharing the rapture with you?

The mentally unbalanced (God bless and heal them) who

hear strange voices telling them that they are Napoleon or Julius Caesar are alone in their hallucinations. You, in your certitude of fellowship with God, are just one in an immense multitude sharing the rapture of hearing God's voice and finding in it the key to the mystery of our lives.

Chapter 3

The Prayer Cell

He bids us build each other up.
—Charles Wesley

A sincere young woman raised the question, "Did we need the Prayer Life Movement?"

We don't resent the question by any means. Any minister or layperson has a natural hesitation about new "movements." Usually this involves more organization, more committees, more correspondence—and they have enough of that already.

When the Women's Fellowship first began to spread through the Methodist church, I sensed this same distaste. Ministers said, "We have our Sisterhoods and Women's Meetings. We will try and make them better if you wish. But why do we want a central organization, district representatives, and all the other rigmarole?" I certainly understood their hesitation, yet I hoped they would come to think that what the women were doing was worth it all.

There is no organization about the Prayer Life Movement, no central committee or district representatives, no correspondence required from the members except an initial postcard. So let us dispose of that bugaboo. Clergy need take no share in it at all, although their leadership or at least their goodwill would be most welcome. But it isn't necessary. People who want to pray together and want instruction in the art of prayer simply register their decision and pray. If we were to have active prayer cells in every Christian home, if the churches could be a cluster of them, if interdenominational groups could spring up in thousands of neighborhoods and businesses, it is impossible to compute all the difference that this would make in society.

Yet the question remains, did we need prayer cells? Everyone must answer that for himself. Let anyone in the pastoral charge of a congregation in any place ponder these questions: Do my people know how to pray? Do they know the range of prayer: adoration, confession, thanksgiving, intercession, petition, meditation? Can they clearly distinguish one from the other, and know how they balance in true prayer? Do they know how to pray for the sick? how to listen to God? how to check the guidance when it comes? how to be obedient? Do they have family prayer in their homes? Does the life of the church center on prayer? Are they planting prayer cells where they work and opening their homes for interdenominational prayer where they live?

If the answer to all these questions is a plain yes, give a cheer—you don't need a prayer movement. Other people may, but you don't. You can ignore it. But if the answer isn't yes, then perhaps a prayer cell is precisely what you need.

Prayer Cells and the Church

Our private prayers are precious. Alone they can meet low-voltage needs. But electric wires multiplied into cables can move buses and trains and illuminate whole cities. That is one reason why we need prayer cells.

It is much easier to overcome your fears and learn the truth about yourself in a loving, prayer-united fellowship than it is on your own. That is another reason why we need prayer cells.

At some churches there is no obvious connection between the prayer cells and the annual business meeting or the leaders' meeting, deacons' meeting, the Session, or the Church Council. Quite often the people who attend one don't belong to the other. One man remarked on this point, "At our church, there's no connection between the boiler and the engine."

In other congregations the influence of prayer cells on the whole church life is quite transforming. Many letters have reported the benefits: "better atmosphere in church," "larger congregations," "more concern for the unchurched," "closer unity of church and Sunday school," "deeper understanding of the minister's task," "our praying has affected our giving," "we have become aggressive in evangelism," "we no longer regard the quality of the preaching as the test of all things," "it is making our church a family," "a new spirit of prayer is permeating our other meetings as well," "we are planning a School of Prayer for the whole church," "our prayer group is our old half-dead prayer meeting reborn— and what a change!"

Notice that phrase "our old half-dead prayer meeting"! Sometimes when we talk to older Christians, their eyes will light up as they describe the prayer meetings they knew when they were young. They will speak nostalgically of the fervor, power, and appeal of those meetings and regretfully assure us that the spiritual life of the church has fallen and withered as the prayer meetings died away.

What Killed the Old Prayer Meetings?

If it is true that the spiritual power of a church depends on the quality of its prayer life, then it is important to know what went wrong. What killed the old prayer meetings? I can give a short, sharp answer to that question, for I am just old enough to remember the old prayer meetings and to have witnessed their passing. The old prayer meetings were killed by the old prayers and by the folk who prayed them.

The prayers had become stale repetitions of what had been said for years, sometimes in exactly the same words. Often they were phrased in obscure biblical language. Sometimes they seemed to claim validity for one particular form of conversion and to deny the reality of any other spiritual experience. Often they were utterances from which passion and living experience had long departed. Sometimes they were clothed with a show of passion that sounded singularly insincere. They became boring. Reality disappeared and the meetings dwindled, leaving the same old faithful few to pray their same old prayers.

Generally, in Great Britain these meetings were held after the Sunday evening service, and those who stayed sometimes regarded themselves as "the elect," the "genuine" Christians. Perhaps unconsciously but often deliberately, they made everybody else feel that by failing to attend, they were lukewarm, second-rate Christians. I have heard tactless prayers for those who had left, which clearly showed this poor opinion of them.

Those who stayed were sometimes (not always, thank God) the most bigoted and censorious of all the members. They never for a moment realized how offensive their bitter self-righteousness was and how effectively it drove the young people away. They never dreamed that many observers said, "If being a Christian means being like them, I want little to do with it." They killed the old prayer meetings all right!

And yet, our urgent need is a return to the prayer meeting. But to the real live prayer meeting, not to the cold and decaying thing so many meetings became.

The essential element about a true and vital prayer meeting is that it should spring spontaneously out of an urgent situation. It should minister to keenly felt needs. The moment it becomes formal, either drop it or revitalize it; otherwise it will rapidly go sour. Do not let it linger on, or it will do more harm than good.

Let me tell you about a real prayer meeting that I knew as a young man. I did not *go* to it; I *belonged* to it. It was part of my life. A dozen boys and I were bound together by invisible but mighty ties. Our leader was an old engineman who worked in the shipyard. He was great in nothing except in soul. Every Friday night we met in a basement. Each week the leader asked one of us to preside, another to give a short ten-minute talk. We began in fear and stuttering, but his wonderful smile carried us on. Yet all this (and it made preachers of some of us) was merely preliminary to the main business of prayer. We longed for the moment when we knelt on the floor, our elbows on our chairs, and one after another poured out our hearts to God. Sometimes between bursts of prayer someone would softly begin some old chorus that caught the mood of our supplication, and at times hearts would melt and tears fall as the warmth of the love of God flowed into us. Sometimes if a lad was in deep trouble—and we were no strangers to sorrow and want in those days—or if we were constrained to lay before God some special concern, then prayer would pour out like a torrent until the very room echoed and shook with the power of pleading.

Prayer meetings of this character require for leader someone who is able to offer encouragement, to guide and direct and point the way to Christ. To everyone else in the church, our old friend was just "Bob Robinson." Few apart from us young men knew him for the spiritual giant he was. But prayer meetings like this teach people how to pray, open to them the life of God, and allow the Holy Spirit to equip them for Christian service.

Such meetings are not usually held on Sunday. I know one or two places where the old-time after-service meeting has retained some of its ancient power, but they are rare. And I fear the real prayer meeting is not likely to be revived in churches where it has died out, or never existed, simply by deciding to start one. Prayer meetings do not begin that way. They begin in hunger for God.

I have known church leaders to decide to begin a prayer meeting more from a sense of duty than passionate conviction. It was duly announced during the evening service, but all who stayed were the few old "faithfuls." Such efforts prove an embarrassment rather than a blessing. It is far better to begin with such a class as I have described, a real prayer group, meeting during the week and not when people are hurrying away from church. And it will probably be better to hold it in somebody's den rather than in a cold and dusty Sunday school room.

Leadership in the Prayer Cell

But let us return for a moment to this all-important matter of the leader. A prayer cell can exist without one, of course. It can be run like an informal committee or just as a group of friends. Such groups can be very pleasant and quite useful, but unless the group is very wide awake, there can be real dangers in amiable improvisation. Without oversight or consistent direction, it can all unconsciously become rather superficial, a flirting with religion rather than working at it. Good leaders will see to it that such pitfalls are avoided. Their job is to make the prayer cell effective.

How do they do it?

First, good prayer leaders must have a great love for people. They must be deeply interested in every member of their cell. This means getting to know them and offering a warm friendliness that draws the best out of them. The leaders must think highly of them, without a spark of condescension, and in their own daily devotions thank God for them. They must see the members as dear to Christ and therefore infinitely dear to them, both for their own sakes and for their Master's.

Strong affection is the indispensable basis of successful prayer leadership. The cold, distant leader who is not really interested in persons simply cannot generate the atmosphere in which people learn the great secrets of prayer. You do not need to be brilliant or learned or cultured to be a great group leader, but you do need a great heart. Remember the leadership of Mr. Greatheart in *The Pilgrim's Progress*.

Next, leaders must prepare for every meeting of the cell. In their private devotions they must intercede for every member of the cell, earnestly seeking the guidance they need. As they pray they will be led to consider what subjects they ought to bring up. These will rise from the situations in which the group members find themselves. Sometimes it will be a problem that is troubling one of them, a temptation to be faced, some estranged relationship at work, some call to service that is being neglected, or some special anxiety such as the illness of a relative or a bereavement.

Again, the leaders should rivet what they have to say in the Scriptures, reading the appropriate verses and giving a very brief exposition. It should rarely be more than a few minutes—five or ten at the most, for the prayer cell is not a study circle or a preaching service. The little talk should lead at once to directed prayer, its whole purpose being to state clearly the objective of the prayers.

Above all, leaders should teach their members how to pray, especially the beginners. These they can encourage by asking them to say just one little sentence on their own or, if they prefer, to repeat some verse from the Bible or from the hymnal that has been of help to them. The leaders must understand the real terror some people feel in speaking in public at all, and how afraid some people are of praying aloud.

The leaders will ask shy persons to write out a prayer of their own composition to be read by them the following week. Soon the leaders will be urging them to venture to pray spontaneously. They may say, "Let us imagine the Lord is here sitting beside me. And He really is here, you know, even if our physical eyes cannot see Him. Now just talk to Him, as if you were talking to me. Don't bother about Thee's and Thou's. Just put your thoughts into words and tell Him as clearly as you can what you feel about this matter."

The leaders' aim is twofold. They have to foster the spiritual development of each member, but they also have to link a cell to the life of the church so that it does not become ingrown, sufficient to itself. This means that they must continually remind the members of the needs of the greater fellowship of the church and make them feel the challenge. It means times of intercession for the church, its ministers and officers, its members and workers, its scholars and youth. The prayer cell is not a cozy and smug retreat for mildly religious folk; it is there to fertilize the church. It generates spiritual vision and power.

Lastly, the leaders' hope is that out of their cells will come other prayer leaders who can gather other cells around them so that prayer cells proliferate. When that happens, the atmosphere of the whole church can change.

Objectives of the Prayer Cells

We believe that prayer cells are a work of the Holy Spirit. As we reflect on the origin and growth of the Prayer Life Movement, it seems that there were three main objectives to which God directed us.

1. To develop the spiritual life of each member

Some years ago a famous leader of the church was contemplating retirement. I knew how busy he had been in the affairs of the church, and I asked him how he intended to occupy himself when he had no office to run, no more committees, no more traveling around the country. He answered, "I shall have time to grow a soul." Sometime later I related this to an old friend, who commented, "He's got a late start, hasn't he?"

It is easy to be busy about so many things and forget this, "the better part." In the prayer cells we begin to cultivate specifically the way of Christ. We examine ourselves before Him; we let His Spirit have His way with us; we take time to be holy.

We are not advocating that spurious and unhealthy kind of introspection that is forever taking itself to pieces and never grows. Rather, we refer to the regular checkup and the sincere effort to put into practice what we learn in the secret place. Everyone should be happier as a result of the cell's steady discipline in prayer. A new warmth and kindness should come into its voice and touch. The love of God that thrills us in the holy moment of prayer should shine through into every daily contact with people.

Remember that spiritually you will either go on, advancing from glory to glory, or you will fall back and swiftly lose what little you have. Conversion is only the beginning. Perfection—Christian perfection—is the end. The goal is to be filled with all the fullness of God, to attain to the stature of Christ.

2. To raise the spiritual life of your church

Do we really know and love the church of God? It is the community of the companions of Jesus. It is the body of Christ.

To every member of the body, the Spirit has given some spiritual gift for the benefit of the whole. He has given a gift to you, not for your own glorification, but for building up the flock of Christ. These gifts are given at the discretion of the Spirit with the needs of the church in view.

We often deplore a shortage of preachers or teachers, visitors, missionaries, administrators, evangelists, ministers, prophets, and stewards. But God has given these gifts. The tragic fact is that often they lie wrapped in a napkin and buried.

We complain at the lack of good preachers. If God has given this gift to you, what have you done with it? We deplore the difficulty of recruiting Sunday school teachers. Who really cares? Some of us have the gift of teaching, but we have been too busy or too idle to teach these lambs of Christ. If our personal piety does not take us into the life of the church, then the Lord will require these sheep at our hand—the sheep that we might have sought and found and kept, but which now are lost. Are we leaving all the work to somebody else?

Then think about your congregation. Is your worship the glorious and splendid praise of God whom you delight to adore with the best you have to offer?

Are the sanctuary windows clean, showing that someone cares? Is the paint fresh and bright, inside and out? If you really love God, can you comfortably plan the decoration of your own home and tolerate a dirty, untidy, and dismal house of God? The world will judge what you think about God by the way you care for your church building. If it means little to you, can you expect it to mean much to them?

What about the finances of God's business? A conversion that stops at the heart and does not reach the pocket will not make a saint or build up the church.

Christian stewardship means giving to God regularly a specified portion of your income, worked out between you and God in prayer. It is a matter for each individual to decide; but it ought to be decided after a full review, not left to occasional spurts of benevolence or the customary collection. Keep a record; balance up at the end of the month, and see how much or how little you have actually given to God.

3. To make you part of God's answer to the world's needs

Personal piety, even the piety that delights in the church, can be blind, unlovely, lopsided, and disappointing to Christ unless it issues in a life of service to mankind. Prayer cells are not escapist; they are not hideouts for those afraid to face life. They are there to help us to equip ourselves to take Christ into our business and our daily work. Christ wants us to surrender every part of life to God.

That means taking Christ into industry—facing the problems of labor relationships, practicing honest dealing at every level, having a concern for the consumer as well as the producer. It means taking Christ into politics—into every party, into local, state, and national government; opinions will differ, but principles remain. It means taking Christ into the universities, colleges, hospitals, racquet clubs; into every association of men and women open to us. It means that the prayer cells should inspire Christian dramatists, artists, poets, novelists, bringing the touch of Christ into every creative activity of the spirit of man. "There is no holiness but social holiness" goes John Wesley's apt phrase.

Keeping the Prayer Cell Healthy

Unless carefully watched, prayer cells, like the old prayer meetings, can become lifeless and superficial and lose their power and purpose. So we must keep our standards high by reminding ourselves exactly what a mature and healthy group can be.

So from time to time, let us submit our cell to a series of searching questions:

(a) Does the cell meet regularly at the appointed time and place? Some people are too casual about their meetings. Serious events may prevent any of us from attending at times or make us late occasionally. But regular carelessness on these matters, especially in the leadership, is bad.

(b) Does the cell have someone who really "cares" for it? He or she need not be the leader, but every group needs someone at its center with a pastoral heart, watching over the members, holding them together, rounding them up, almost playing the sheepdog to the flock.

If someone remarks, "People who need rounding up can't be very committed," the answer is that none of us is always at our best. If we were allowed to slip away in the first chill that nips our enthusiasm, we would fail in most of the things we have attempted for God.

(c) Is the cell fused together in a deep, divinely given love? We think a dozen is an ideal maximum for a group, because it is hard for everybody to know everybody at any depth if the numbers get large. Fourteen or sixteen may be no problem, but experience seems to point to the wisdom of forming new cells as the numbers grow. Start the new cell off with some of your most mature members, but see to it that each cell is a living unity with love at its heart and circumference.

(d) Does the cell's prayer extend beyond itself? There must be local needs for prayer that only you can know. But if you neglect to pray for concerns beyond your own congregation, you limit fellowship and can become too parochial. A sense of unity with Christians at large is very important. (See the next chapter regarding "prayer objectives.")

(e) Is your cell rich in intercessors? Powerful intercessors are still rare, as in Isaiah's day: "And he . . . wondered that there was no intercessor" (Isa. 59:16). People need help through prayer the most at times when they are least capable of it—in lashing pain, in appalling weariness, in great sorrow, or in a muddled state of mind. The intercessor is so full of love that he can place himself between the infinite power of God and the piteous human need. He can become a channel of love, peace, patience, courage—all that the storm-tossed soul needs.

To be willing to give time daily to intercession is lovely service. No one may know of it but God. Yet the men and women who practice it are people who affect the future.

Searching Questions About Prayer

We have indicated that a prayer cell session should begin with a brief consideration of one or other of the problems of prayer, directed toward the deepening of prayer experience. But the prayer cell must not be turned into a discussion group; the purpose is to drive a point home, to teach another lesson in the art and craft of prayer. Sometimes such consideration can gather naturally around a searching question. Here are a few practical examples. Wise leaders will collect dozens of them as they listen to the confidence of their members.

—What do you think is the best definition of prayer?
—How do you distinguish affirmative prayer from petition?
—Why is it very important to think before you pray?
—Is there such a thing as "unanswered" prayer?
—To what thoughts does your mind normally turn when you are not thinking of anything in particular?
—Someone has said, "No holiness without prayer; no revival without prayer; no mastery of life without prayer." Do you agree? Explain.
—A man said, "I pray, but I always have to push myself to it. How can I love prayer?" What advice would you give him?
—A housewife inquires, "Is washing up a good time for extra moments of prayer?" Answer her.

—A student asks, "Is it right to pray about exams?" Give a thoughtful reply.
—Is there risk in prayer?
—Are you prepared to see yourself in Christ?
—Are you ready to be made honest "in the inward parts"?
—Can you say (and mean), "Create in me a clean heart, O God"?
—Do you want purity of heart before everything else?
—Are you trying to use prayer just to get things?
—When we listen, God speaks. Are you ready to obey?

Many groups keep minutes of things prayed for. The practice has a threefold use: (a) it helps precision in prayer aims, (b) it guards against casual, around-the-world, what-have-you praying, and (c) it permits a periodic check on answers.

We commend this practice as long as the "secretary" resists all temptations to write up a romantic story. The record should be factual, humble, and utterly sincere, without trimmings. It may be best to keep it as a kind of diary, not to be read and confirmed at the next meeting, but preserved in secret until it is wanted. Our prayers are for God and to God, not primarily for human record. They are recorded elsewhere in another Book.

Chapter 4

Prayer Cell Objectives

I notice that if I am praying for my friends, coincidences happen; if I stop praying for my friends, the coincidences stop.

—William Temple

The Prayer Cell Movement has had two sources of strength. It is both combined prayer and directed prayer.

When we join with others, our loneliness and isolation are broken down. It is a wonderful comfort to find other men and women who are facing the same problems, carrying the same loads, fighting the same temptations. To hear someone else pray the same prayer that we have poured out can of itself bring relief. To meet the same Lord together and to feel the common ties of intimate discipleship strengthen our faith and assurance.

Yet members of a prayer cell not only pray together, but also pray with the same objectives. They know that other Christians are praying with them with these same purposes in mind. That is why a prayer cell needs objectives. Aimless prayer is like small talk, ambling and meandering but getting nothing done. Prayer must be directed to be effective.

The Concerns of the Prayer Cell

Members of the Prayer Cell Movement pledge themselves to regular prayer, for intermittent, occasional prayer is as useless as intermittent, occasional efforts to play the piano. This regular prayer moves over three broad areas of concern: self, others, and the world.

Self comes first because we cannot help but begin with ourselves. We are the persons praying. But self is not to be the center of our attention. It must be very firmly handled. True prayer will reveal much that is wrong with self and in need of correction. Nor must concern with self be permitted to degenerate into an obsession with our sins and faults. The objective for self is quite clear. It is the positive aim that our experience of Christ may become as fresh as the air we breathe, that we may have this communion with Him now, and that we may go on to know Him better.

Second, we pray for others, and this is more important than praying for oneself. Our objective is not that others may secure this favor or that blessing or be saved from some particular trouble, though we shall raise all these concerns in prayer. Rather, the great end is that they may come to know Christ and enter into the fellowship of His church. The whole burden of our intercession is that we may share Christ's concern for them. To fail to pray for our neighbors and friends and for those known to us would be a disastrous denial of love. "Moreover as for me, God forbid that I should sin against the LORD in ceasing to pray for you" (1 Sam. 12:23).

Third, we must pray for the world, especially for a worldwide spiritual awakening in our time. Everyone longs for peace and security from the threat of war; we must pray that the continuing peace of Christ may become the peace of the whole world. And this involves a new world order of justice in which poverty, disease, ignorance, and vice must be eradicated.

All our concerns can be mustered under these general categories. The prayer cell objectives are not intended to confine the range or the particularity of our petitions. They provide the shared framework of our combined intercessions. Let us examine them a little more closely.

Self

We have put self first because we begin with ourselves, but its real place in the life of prayer is last. Selfishness in prayer is abominable. Self is the battlefield, and self must be subdued by every prayer warrior. But to do that successfully you must oust self from the center of the picture and enthrone Christ Jesus there instead. So be careful how you handle self in prayer. Put self last and least.

Before you begin to pray for yourself, be quiet before God. Then ask yourself what you would like most for yourself. Clear your mind. Reject every unworthy suggestion, however plausible, that would not bear the scrutiny of the Crucified. Keep searching until you find one great personal need—something so harmonious with Christ's Spirit that it can be prayed for *in His Name.* It may well be something like this: a longing for more Christlike love; a longing to be filled with the Holy Spirit; a longing to make progress in prayer. Remember, when self is on the throne of your heart, Christ is on the Cross; when self is on the cross, Christ is on the throne.

Others

When you leave the battle for the soul and pray for others, you enter the wonderful and tender ministry of intercession. Start with your friends. They are among your greatest treasures. Friends are sometimes nearer, dearer, and closer than relatives. Most of us would hate to fail our friends, but we fail our friends most tragically if, in the time of their great need, we fail to pray for them with persistence, concentration, and great compassion.

Most of us have some friends to whom religion means little or nothing. Pray that God may become real to them. Pray that there may be some quality in your own life which will make them know without any preaching by you that "there is something in religion after all."

This illustrates, incidentally, the proper way to pray for oneself—indirectly, in order that we may serve others. We sanctify ourselves for their sakes, not our own. This leads us to think about our churches.

Let us meditate unhurriedly on the needs of our own congregations. Let us not accuse other people in our hearts. *They* might be different if *we* were. Let us love them. Now let us wait on God—just wait, thinking of God and the church. Ask Him, "What is our deepest local need, Father?" Is it for more prayer, more God-centeredness, more concern about the unchurched in the neighborhood, more contact between church and Sunday school, more glad attendance at Communion? Whatever it is, pray for that.

Only the minister knows all the demands on his time. Only the minister knows how far he falls beneath his own ideals, not to mention his Lord's. No church cell will forget to intercede for its minister and for the spiritual life of the local church. Pray for the minister. Pray for all in office in the local church. Pray for the Sunday school teachers.

It is wise to think about the whole life of the church, to list its needs carefully, and then to pray for each concern separately. If the leader introduces each theme and calls for prayer, we can all utter our own thoughts and insights, and by this loving pleasure our own hearts are moved to do what lies in our power. Take time over it.

Here is an example of such a list. Let us intercede:

—For all the infants on the nursery roll whom we see no more in our churches. May God show us what negligent shepherds we are.

—For all Sunday school students who drift away from us. May His Spirit show us our failure to seek the lost children.

—For the youth who come to our clubs but have no time for the church. May God help us to see ourselves as they see us.

—For the mothers who come to our women's meetings but cannot come on Sundays. May God help us to care for them and nourish them in the faith.

—For the women who worship with us on Sundays whose husbands and children never come. May God teach us to help them win their families for Christ.

—For older folk and shut-ins who cannot come to church and are sometimes forgotten and neglected by the congregation they have served.

—For those who attend church but have no glowing experience, who value the fellowship of men but know not the fellowship of the Holy Spirit, who love the church buildings but not the church of Christ. May God show us what the church really is.

—For those who have ceased to meet with us, whose first love has grown cold, who love this present world rather than the kingdom. May God reveal to us how weak were the ties of our love that could let them go so easily.

—For this generation that has discarded religion and measures all things by material standards. May God reveal to us the way to their hearts, disclosing to us how much littleness and false religiosity have robbed our spiritual life of any real value or attraction.

O Lord Jesus Christ, who is the Head of the church, which is Your body, forgive our blindness, our complacency, and our unwillingness to be disturbed. Give us caring hearts. Teach us how to seek the lost with love and understanding. Show us how much we are to blame for their going astray, and help us to learn of You, so that with Your wisdom and love we may not rest until we have sought and found another for You, for Your name's sake, Amen.

The Whole Church

But the local church is not the whole church, and we are poor Christians if our horizon is bounded by the four walls of our own beloved Bethel. It becomes then a prison for the soul instead of a ladder to heaven. Think of the great church, the bride of Christ.

The church has many faults. It has much to repent of. There are stains on its history. We have fallen far short of the challenge of the gospel and have not been a light to people who have not yet really seen the Light of the World.

Christendom is divided. Some Christians think the divisions are a sin and some think that God can use these divisions in the high strategy of heaven. Whatever the truth about that is, God cannot use the coldness and contempt that sometimes marks the manner, thought, and comments by one group of Christians toward another. This appalling lack of love hinders the purposes of God and only helps the forces of evil.

Love can live and grow even where people do not see Truth in the same light nor explain their experience in the same way. Nothing excuses Christians for failure in love—for God is Love.

Make a practice of learning more about people in other Communions—what they believe and why, how they worship and why. Learn—in order to love more. Admire wherever you can. Praise what you admire. Pray for your own cherished Communion. Pray for other branches of Christendom. Pray that we may draw closer to each other in love. Pray for penitence and humility in the church. Pray for all Christians (missionaries and non-missionaries) in non-Christian lands, that they may shine with the life of Christ.

The World

And so we think of the great world outside the church, the world which God loves and which He sent His Son to redeem.

We appear to be at a fateful period in world history. People have often thought that, but not on such good grounds as we. We could stumble into nuclear holocaust, or we could scale the height that leads to the throne of God. Much depends on a comparatively small group of men—the premier of the Soviet Union, the President of the United States, the prime minister of Great Britain, and a few others. We know something of each of them—their names, aims, responsibilities. Let us picture them. Let us enter as completely as we can into their position. Let us think on God and His purposes in the world.

We see suspicion, hate, envy, and the threat of war. Let us pray for understanding, trust, cooperation, and peace.

It would be good if we occasionally focused on one particular country or continent for special prayer. Africa is the continent where Christianity is spreading the fastest at this time. Throbbing with new life, thick with enormous problems, the most lovely and the most awful things could happen in Africa in the decades to come. Pray for African political leaders. Pray for all who are working for the reconciliation of the races. Pray for Christian leaders of all races in Africa.

Completing Prayer

One final word: the objectives are aims, but prayer must clothe them with words and power. There is a danger that all our prayer time may be given to intercession and petition. The heroes of faith of the past gave most of their prayer time to adoration. Let us never forget it in our cells, nor forget its priority. Adore God! Just sit in your group in silent contemplation of the great One who made us, maintains us, came to us in Jesus, and lives within us in the power and person of the Holy Spirit. Be glad when you find yourself "lost in wonder, love, and praise." Such time is never "lost." An adoring awareness of God is by far the best preparation for every other part of prayer.

After adoration should come confession. Do the members of the prayer cell have anything to confess? Is it worth going over the check list (ch. 3)?

Thanksgiving should find its place in every prayer. Talk about and list the matters for gratitude:

—Personal petitions answered?
  (a) a tenderer conscience about animals?
  (b) more help given to refugees?
  (c) anti-Semitism abating?
—What has given you special happiness about your local church?
—Are the sick for whom you are praying better, braver, more open to God?
—The shadows over the world seem in some ways to grow darker, the problems more acute. Yet there are things to be glad about even now. Name them. Thank God.
—Let the cell quietly assess the present prospects for world peace. What are you deeply glad about? Be thankful.

Then move on to your intercessions for others, the church, and the world. Never omit the local needs that God has laid on your hearts.

Conclude with a note of praise. Bless God for Himself. Delight in His being, and magnify the Lord. Let your last thoughts be of Him.

Chapter 5

The Perils of Prayer

O Lord, all our ills come from not fixing our gaze on Thee: if we looked at nothing else but where we are going we should arrive, but we fall a thousand times and stumble and stray because we do not keep our eyes bent on Him who is the Way. —St. Teresa

There are dangers in the life of prayer, pitfalls into which the unwary can easily stumble. Without noticing it, the beginner can acquire slovenly habits of devotion that will defeat him in the end. Times of special difficulty will surely come, and we must know how to handle them, so that nothing is allowed to deflect or hinder us from our goal, which is unbroken communion with God.

The Danger of Relying on Feelings

First and commonest, there is the natural tendency to rely on feelings. The first moments of prayer to a newly awakened soul can be a joyful and thrilling experience. But later, when the emotional reaction has set in, prayer often becomes lifeless, dull, and unreal. God no longer feels near. One of the primary lessons of prayer is to learn that we must keep on praying whether we feel God or not.

It is not that God withdraws Himself from us. He is just as

near; He fills all time and space. The causes of this dryness or aridity are well understood. Here are the possibilities:

1. Is there some flaw in my soul to which God is pointing? Is He asking me to deal with some temper in which I like to indulge? If there is, then I cannot expect God to visit my soul with glimpses of His presence till I have dealt with the ulcerating spot. The way through is a severe and honest self-examination in the sight of God, followed by repentance and forgiveness. Only the saints know how many struggles and tears mark the path of prayer.

2. Is there some job the Lord wants me to do that I am reluctant to undertake? Am I settled and comfortable and unwilling to be disturbed? It is easy to love God and delight in His will when what He wants is what we want; it is terribly difficult to break with loved associations and to travel on some road from which our whole being rebels. Yet to every Christian comes this moment, not just once, but many times, when self-will and personal preference must be firmly put to one side and the hard, cruel, and unlovely cross taken up.

Yet, as long as we refuse to stoop to that cross, God cannot and will not give any more of Himself, and the little we have will soon be lost. The warm companionship for which we long will be ours again only when we say, "Not my will, but Thine, be done."

3. The aridity may be due neither to sin nor to disobedience, but simply to God's intention to toughen our spiritual muscles. Faith must never rest on anything so transient as feelings; it must depend, not on us, but on God. He wants us to learn how to pray and believe even when we feel nothing. We must never pray for or strive after feelings, for these sensations are not an end in themselves. They accompany certain phases of divine intervention, but the end of prayer is the vision of God, and for that one must be pure in heart; hence the discipline and purifying action of

the dry periods. So thank God for your feelings, and thank Him too when you feel nothing.

This, by the way, is the real answer to those who dismiss prayer as an illusion, a form of auto-suggestion or self-deception. The searching of the heart, the acceptance of a deeper challenge, the willingness to go the way of the Cross—these are not the marks of someone who is escaping from reality; these are the signs of spiritual growth.

The Danger of Wandering Thoughts

Second, there is the peril of wandering thoughts. Do you find it hard to concentrate in prayer? Does your mind wander in spite of all your efforts? Do the events and memories of the day crowd in as you try to listen to God? Do you sometimes feel that you cannot go on, that it is useless to keep on trying? Don't be alarmed. Everybody beginning the life of prayer knows this experience. We should expect it and be prepared for it.

Saints of old were well aware of it. St. Nilus, in his "Treatise on Prayer," says, "The Devil is very envious of the man who prays and uses all possible means to defeat his purpose without ceasing, suggesting thoughts to his memory, and endeavouring to excite his carnal passions, so that, if possible, he may prevent his ascent to God." When a man commits himself to prayer, he begins a spiritual warfare; he wrestles not against flesh and blood, but against the foes of the soul.

There is another reason for wandering thoughts, especially in the early stages of the prayer life. Until the Spirit has made us whole—until, that is, we are sanctified—our personalities are disorganized. Tempers, passions, and emotions are ill-controlled. The mind resents being held too closely to one subject. In prayer we are learning how to harness our minds and bring them under the yoke of Christ so that we can put them at God's disposal.

So when your thoughts wander at prayer, do not panic, and above all do not stop praying. Make the incident a steppingstone to bring you nearer God. You cannot help it when fascinating ideas and images flash into your consciousness, distracting your mind and heart from God; but as soon as you realize what is happening, return to God as quickly as you can and say, "See, Lord, this is the kind of person You have condescended to love. Here I am, undisciplined, unreliable, the easy victim of every scatterbrained thought. Be patient with me, Lord, and let me resume our business where we were before this interruption."

As we persist we shall find the distractions waning. Part of our soul will be on the lookout for them and warn us of their coming. That is why the Lord Jesus repeatedly urges us to "watch and pray." We can't continue in prayer without watching. We may close our physical eyes to keep out the distracting sights of this world, but it is fatal to close our spiritual eyes. They must always be open for all the subtle assaults that would deflect us from communion with God.

So be on your guard constantly. Nothing will more quickly destroy your love of prayer and keep you from God than wandering thoughts. You must learn to control, direct, and discipline your mind as surely as a great artist controls the hand that holds his brush.

The Danger of Weariness

Third, there is the danger of weariness. You can't pray well when you're weary. The tired mind can say "thank you" and ask a general blessing on all and sundry, but it cannot scale the mount of God. Prayer is the exploration of the unseen; one needs to be alert with a keen watchfulness. Remember the Master's admonition: "Watch and pray."

There are times when God understands and forgives our weariness. We offer it to Him. But to leave prayer until we are tired out is folly indeed. The jaded mind cannot distinguish clearly between truth and error. It is neither receptive nor alert. Weariness robbed the disciples of fellowship with Christ when He needed them most, in the Garden of Gethsemane.

So choose carefully the time you set aside for prayer. If you can make it first thing in the morning, so much the better. If not, keep some moments while you are fresh and efficient for this strenuous practice of prayer.

Avoid erratic prayer. Fix the hour and stick to it. Keep your appointment. Only extreme emergency should be allowed to cancel or postpone the time of prayer. We owe punctuality to the Majesty who deigns to receive us. We need the discipline of regular prayer just as a plant needs regular watering and feeding. Haphazard prayer is usually shallow. Only regular prayer digs deep channels.

The Danger of Overtalking

Fourth, we can talk so much to God that prayer becomes a drug; it ought to be a stimulant. We can fly to prayer to escape reality; it ought to help us to face reality—not only the harsh aspects of society, but unpleasant truths about ourselves. We may drown the voice of God by our incessant chatter, our nonstop spate of words. We must avoid the peril of much speaking.

Prayer means listening as well as talking, but it is easier to talk than to listen. To listen you must hold the spirit poised in quietness; you must restrain the quick movement of the mind that flies like a shuttle from one thought to another. You must firmly bring it back to the question, What is God saying to me?

You may not find it easy at first. The mind races and prances like an untrained colt, but to be of any use it must be harnessed and must learn to be controlled. "Be still and know that I am God" is one of the great laws of prayer. You must learn how to be still.

The hidden motive behind this compulsive talking is the secret fear of what God might say to us. We do not want to hear His challenge and rebuke. Yet if we do not listen to His words, we shall miss all that He wants to give us.

So when you pray, allow pauses. Alternate speech with silence. In that way prayer will be a dialogue, not a monologue; a conversation, not a soliloquy.

Let the spoken part be direct, simple, and sincere. Let the silence be rich with wonder and worship. The hushed moments of self-examination are just as much prayer as the utterance of praise and petition. As you learn to value the mystery of silence, the quietness of God will bring peace to your soul.

The Danger of Giving Up

Fifth, there is the danger of giving up because there seems to be no real answer to our prayer. This peril is so grave that when Jesus gave His disciples their lesson in prayer and taught them that great outline that we call the Lord's Prayer, He went on immediately to warn them of this particular peril (Luke 11:5-13).

Jesus told the disciples a story—a somewhat amusing little incident that had a deadly serious intent. He put it into the form of a question to make quite sure that each man applied it to himself. He asked, "Which of you shall have a friend, and shall go unto him at midnight, and shall say unto him, Friend, lend me three loaves; for a friend of mine in his journey is come to me, and I have nothing to set before him?" (vv. 5-6).

The man of the story is a friendly man. One of his friends has been overtaken by night in his journey and has dropped in on him without warning, catching him entirely unprepared; his cupboard is empty. But he is not dismayed. He has another friend, easily accessible, who always has enough and to spare, and in the sure confidence of old and tried friendship he hurries over to his home and knocks on the door, even though it is midnight.

Here is a man rich in friends. An unfriendly Christian is a contradiction in terms. The road of friendship is the open path to every man's heart. The cold, reserved, and friendless heart lives in frigid isolation. So unless our faith makes us ever more friendly, there is something seriously amiss with our prayer life.

This friendly man discovered late one night that he had nothing to offer the traveler in need. This is the picture of the disciple to whom the hungry world turns for help. In ourselves and by ourselves, we have nothing to offer. We cannot save the world. By ourselves we cannot satisfy anyone who is hungering and thirsting after righteousness, though we often try in our self-sufficiency. We offer our human wisdom and such neighborly help as we can, but the deep needs remain unfilled.

But this friendly man is not beaten. He too has a Friend, and what a Friend! In confidence he hurries and knocks on the door, explains his predicament, and asks for bread, the Bread of life. Then he meets this strange, unfriendly rebuff. The door remains shut, and the only reply he gets is a gruff command to "go away" and to stop making a nuisance of himself.

This is a true picture of prayer. Many times you can go to your Friend, and He will give you anything. But there are times—sometimes occasions of real and desperate emergency—when the door of heaven is sealed and it seems that God is asleep and does not want to be disturbed. Such experiences can occur when we are most anxious that God should help, not just for our own sakes, but for others'.

Here Jesus is warning His disciples to be ready for the bitter experience of the unanswered prayer, and His instruction is quite simple: "Keep on praying." Even if the man inside the house will not get up for friendship's sake, if you keep on knocking long enough, he will get up in sheer desperation to stop your knocking. Pray like that, says Jesus. Keep on praying. "Ask, and it shall be given you; seek, and ye shall find; knock, and it shall be opened unto you" (v. 9).

Then why delay? Does God require long persuasion before He will move to our aid? Is He unwilling to help, and have we to make Him change His mind? Not at all. He is our heavenly Father. He waits to bless, and the cause of the delay lies not in Him but in us and our world. He will pour out His blessing in His own good time—not a moment too soon, not a second late.

Sometimes the delay is needed to allow other factors in our great, complex universe to come together. There is always in the Bible a sense of the fullness of time—that is, the moment of full tide, which has to be seized. God, who alone knows all the facts and who operates through many lives, will keep us waiting until the right moment.

Every great revival has been preceded by periods of intensive, agonizing prayer, when the faithful pleaded with God to pour out His Spirit again and to revive the work. The Welsh Revival of 1904–6 was preceded by ten years of such prayer in cottages and chapels. The movement gathered in intensity through those long years of constant, apparently unanswered prayer until at last it burst into flame in the heart of Evan Roberts.

Today a hungry world has lost its way. Those who know and love its men and women do not deceive themselves into thinking that they have the answer. We are powerless until the Spirit comes upon us; our words and works are ineffective until our Pentecost. And so the great, age-old prayer has begun to go up again: "Lord, send the Spirit."

Jesus said, with gentle irony, that God will not mock you. He will not put you off with something that looks like bread but isn't, something that looks like a fish but is instead a dangerous reptile, or something that looks like an egg but is really a scorpion ready to strike. His gifts will not destroy us, though they may destroy our little preconceptions, our narrowness and bigotries, our selfishness and pride. No, says Jesus, do not be afraid of the gift that will eventually come, for if you know how to give good gifts to your children, how much more—how very much more!—will your heavenly Father give the Holy Spirit to those who ask Him.

I wonder if God did not raise up the Prayer Cell Movement throughout the world to begin this arduous vigil of unceasing prayer once more. It may be soon, it may be years, before the great outpouring comes; but if we believe and keep on praying, if we allow the probing Spirit of God to have His way in our hearts and in our churches, to cleanse and strengthen, then it will surely come, for He who promised is faithful.

The Danger of False Spirituality

Sixth, there is the danger of a false spirituality that can lead to that caricature of faith, "feather-bed Christianity."

Someone wrote to me to question the common injunction that prayer should always be offered on one's knees. Apart from the fact that such a position is physically impossible in many of our church buildings and for many people at home who are crippled and ill, he argued that surely the supremely important thing about prayer is not the attitude of the body, but the attitude of mind and soul. He quoted a much-loved minister who slightly shocked him when he claimed, "My most valuable times of prayer are just before getting out of bed in the morning; with my body perfectly relaxed, my spirit has full play for all the lovely experiences that true prayer can offer." The writer said that almost reluctantly he tried this method and found it worked gloriously, giving him a half-hour of joyous inspiration and sending him into his workday and out into the world with a hymn of praise on his lips and in his heart.

I am sure that in this age of stress and strain we have to learn how to relax—and it is not easy. Many of us sleep with our muscles still taut from the tensions of the day. Yet complete relaxation is wonderfully restful and essential in a fully active life.

To use the interval between waking and rising for the purposes of prayer is both wise and rewarding; it employs the mind and soul while the body relaxes. So also there are times when we cannot sleep, and then it is good to fix our thoughts on God. The psalmist knew this experience.

> My mouth praises thee with joyful lips,
>   when I think of thee upon my bed,
>   and meditate on thee in the watches of the night.
> (Ps. 63:5–6 RSV)

But there are perils of the soul in this practice unless we watch it carefully.

It is a profound mistake to assume that the attitude of the body doesn't matter. The human personality is a unity of body, mind, and soul. The supreme error of Greek philosophy that has influenced so much Western thinking was to divorce body from mind and soul and to regard it as an inferior, mortal, and material envelope in which the immortal soul is imprisoned. Bible teaching flatly opposes this view. The Jews could not conceive of any satisfactory life, now or hereafter, without a body of some kind. That is why Christians hold to the resurrection of the body—although, as Paul insists, it will be a spiritual body adapted to the conditions of that future life. But we shall have a body, because we as humans are incomplete without it. So when we pray, it is the whole man—not just mind and soul, but also the body—that prays, and the attitude of the body indicates the attitude of the whole personality.

When this happens, the life of prayer ranges over all our

dealings with God. There will be times when we can relax in His presence, and moments of physical relaxation afford excellent opportunities for quiet unhurried thought on holy things. If the mind were not occupied with these high tasks, it would latch onto something else. But contemplating God is not just musing and thinking beautiful thoughts while we lie luxuriating in a warm and comfortable bed. Prayer is often a searing experience that drags us to the floor in self-loathing or twists us in an agony of intercession. Prayer that would scale the Mount of God is an arduous and costly experience that at its severest can make our protesting body sweat blood, as Jesus discovered.

So while we can and should use moments of relaxation for holy meditation, let us recognize their limitations in the life of prayer. Lying in bed can never be a substitute for the worship given by the whole man, kneeling or prostrate in adoration before the awful, glorious majesty of God.

The Danger of Complacency

Seventh, there is the danger of complacency. Are you pleased with your prayer cell? Does it thrill the soul? Good! Thank God for it! But beware also. It is at such a moment that the Evil One whispers the deadly suggestion that you and your friends are "pretty good Christians," a lot more sincere than those others who never go to a prayer meeting and wouldn't know how to pray in public if you asked them. The Deceiver will tell you that you are making good progress and you are getting stronger in the faith, so your opinion about church affairs is really important. He will say to you that because you are a lover of prayer, you are a good judge of other people and your criticism of their weaknesses is sound.

So you may find yourself looking down on other people from a spiritual pinnacle, convinced that you are obviously superior. And pride, the deadliest of all sins, has stolen into your heart and made it a living tomb in which faith will die.

Remember that the path of true prayer does not bring this feeling of self-importance. On the contrary, it leads to an increasing sense of our own unworthiness. We become less and less inclined to condemn other people.

> The secret pride, the subtle sin,
> O let it never more steal in,
> To offend Thy glorious eyes.

The Danger of Undisciplined Pity

Eighth, there is the peril of undisciplined pity. Pity is a precious thing that speaks of deep feeling, kind feeling, sympathy, and service. But it is subject to certain serious diseases, and because it relates to prayer we ought to look at them.

It can become self-pity. The emotion that should motivate us to service to others can turn in and curdle inside us. It is dreadful to live with someone who is a martyr to self-pity, who is continually moaning and asking, "Why should this happen to me?" Their need may be real and acute, and why they should have to endure such difficulty and suffering may be a dark mystery; but their self-pity makes it worse. I exhort all members of a prayer group (especially those with a burden to bear) to fight self-pity as they would fight the plague.

A second disease of pity results from its mingling with pride. Some people seem incapable of feeling pity without feeling superior too. They meet a deaf man or a lame man, and their regret is shot through and through with a sense that they are something better than this poor mortal. A sick woman had a visitor who had not seen her for some time and had not observed the changes the sickness had wrought in her. The visitor went around their circle of friends afterward, saying, "You ought to see her. She is a pitiable object."

"Pitiable?" What an offensive form of pity! "Object"? Just an object—though she was dear enough for Christ to shed His blood for her. When pride mingles with your pity, it has gone bad.

The third disease of pity is its failure to move the will. Pity is one of God's springs of action in the soul; it is meant to motivate us to service—to prayer, to deeds, to help. Yet it often fails in this. People sometimes wallow in pity and don't do a thing about it: "Oh, those poor refugees! Oh, those poor blind children!" Intelligent and persistent prayer is service and leads to other service. So how's your pity?

The Danger of Self-Deception

Ninth, there is always the terrible danger of self-deception. We should derive no particular pleasure from the growing number of prayer cells if we did not feel that they were helping their members to a better understanding of prayer—what it really means, how limited some views of it undoubtedly are, how blind praying people sometimes appear to important aspects of prayer, how useless it would be to add to the millions of people who pray if they were still praying in a blind way.

This truth was brought home to me when a friend reminded us that people could pray for years and still remain blind to their own awful egotism or temper or jealousy or greed or pride. For some reason God never seemed able to get through to their need, was never able to awaken their honest self-consciousness, was never able to show them what everyone else knew about them. "If prayer can't help them," my friend said, "what is the good of saying that prayer is the answer to all our needs?"

But prayer can help them—true prayer. We have never defended the praying that was all human talk and all personal petition. We have said, "If you have only ten minutes for prayer, give six to listening." No prayer will enrich our family life, revive the church, change the nation, and affect the world except the right prayer. If the Prayer Life Movement had gotten bogged down at the level of praying that tries to make God the accomplice of our own selfishness, that would have spoiled it all. From all the evidence, it didn't. But in case anyone is unaware of the danger we are referring to, let us give some illustrations of how we can pray sincerely, persistently, passionately—yet lose our way.

1. A devout woman, still young, quarreled with her sister-in-law five years ago. She is regular and sincere in her praying and does not forget her sister-in-law either. She beseeches God to "change" her sister-in-law, but after all this time the situation has hardened and is seemingly unsolvable, and it looks like another case in the large file of unanswered prayers.

"In-laws" are often congenial, but they can be difficult too. I know this woman's sister-in-law and consider her difficult in some ways; to dismiss the quarrel as 50–50 would be too glib. Maybe it is 70–30! And it gets worse.

Unbelievers know of this situation and smile. I believe God has been seeking to put this right for five years, mainly through the Christian. After all, she prays. But she doesn't listen enough, nor is she skilled in selecting God's voice from the others inside her. From something she once said, I came to think that God wants her to drop her insistence that her sister-in-law "must speak first," and she herself must take the initiative, apologize for the part that was her fault (even if it was the smaller), and not call it the "smaller" in doing so. "What is the use of prayer without listening and obedience?" asked a friend of mine. What indeed?

2. A church official gives all his leisure time to ministry in the congregation. How he works for the place! I believe the

people who say it would close without him. He loves every brick in the building. He gives time, thought, and money to it, and it is sad that it continues to wane. I cannot doubt that he is a man of prayer; it would be offensive to suppose anything else. If anything did make one wonder on the point, it would be his sharp and sometimes contemptuous references to the people in a neighboring church which, it had been suggested (with good reason), should merge with his congregation. "Never!" he says quite firmly, and he means what he says.

I can easily understand that a man may honestly oppose any move to close his church. I believe, even if denominational officials disagree, that he could be right. What I can't understand in a praying man is the lack of love, pride expressing itself in contempt, and the assumption that no one (not even God) could change his mind. Is he listening when he prays? Could it be the will of God that the congregations merge?

3. But enough of other people's sins. Let me confess my own. Soon after going into Germany at the end of World War I, I was promoted to sergeant and put virtually in charge of my platoon. We were instructed to occupy a small German town thirty kilometers from Cologne. The people were starving, and my men took advantage of this. A dreadful number of women were selling their bodies for bread, and the only thing that seemed plentiful was wine. Half the men were drunk night after night. Within six weeks I lost two corporals to venereal disease, and several of the men for the same reason. I stormed and raged (and prayed in a way) and things only got worse. One of my duties was to see that the known prostitutes were submitting themselves for regular medical examination—and I was only nineteen myself!

Most of the men were young soldiers, but among the senior men was a good fellow we all liked, and he asked me to go for a walk with him one night. Well, it's an army rule (or was) that sergeants could only be friends with sergeants, corporals with corporals, and so on; but I was very lonely and low-spirited, so when Harry asked me to go for a walk, I said yes.

During the walk, Harry said, "I suppose you know you are the most hated man in the platoon."

"I suppose I am," I said, "but I don't care. Who would want the affection of that drunken bunch of fornicators?"

"Christ would," Harry said. I grew quiet. "Look, Sergeant," he continued, "I'm a lot older than you, and I'm a Christian too. You're going about this ugly situation the wrong way."

"Tell me the right way," I said a little wearily.

"There's nothing they hate about you so much as your 'p.i.' [platoon instruction] talks. It gets their guts." (Harry wasn't using the language of the prayer cells!) "They'll do nothing you want them to do until they like you, and they'll never like you until you like them."

He said much else, and the only good word I have for myself is that I took it meekly. We walked back to my billet in silence, and it was a long time before I slept. I kept wondering whether I should pray about it more, but I'd been praying so hard (in a way) already. I went to sleep resolved to take it up with God again the next day. I did. It was one of the most dramatic and power-charged interviews I ever had with heaven. God confirmed all that Harry said, and then some! It seems He had been wanting to make His mind clear to me on that subject for a long time.

I went to work on the problem the very next night. Harry and I put the drunks to bed, and I didn't lash them with my tongue. I recalled advantages I had grown up with that most of them didn't have, and I asked God to help me love them.

As honest affection came into my heart, all changed. The men turned to me for counsel. (I even wrote out the love letters of one illiterate.) They sometimes followed my advice.

A few came to the Christian Fellowship I ran. When I was mustered out—earlier than most of them in order to go to college—they seemed sincerely sad to see me go.

There's prayer and there's prayer. We want the real thing, with listening and obedience too.

The Danger of Exhibitionism

Tenth, there is the peril of exhibitionism. There are some people who love to pray aloud in prayer meetings, but who are unconsciously wanting to display their fluency and eloquence rather than to intercede with God.

In the book *Fame Is the Spur*, Howard Spring creates a character called Birley Artingstall. Birley was a kindly man in many ways, but he was of the type I describe. He belonged to Emmot St. Wesleyan Chapel and used to sit through the evening service waiting for the prayer meeting and the minister's request: "Perhaps Brother Birley Artingstall will lead us to the mercy seat."

Spring writes,

> His voice began with cool and reasonable suggestions to a Deity not beyond the reach of common sense and gathered in a few dutiful "Amens." Stage by stage it reached at last a thunderous utterance which culminated invariably in a command to the Lord to come quickly and "sway the sceptre of universal dominion." The fervent "Hallelujahs" that fell like bouquets round Birley Artingstall as he sat down made all but the most obdurate hesitant to follow him. He was always anxious and restless, once the prayer meeting had broken up, until someone had said to him: "You led us tonight with great acceptance." Then he would go happily home.

Without being too severe on anyone, let us admit that this is not real prayer; this is exhibitionism. Birley had his reward. Let us admit also that this had its part in killing the old-time prayer meeting. People don't like this kind of showing-off. Even if they were charitable enough not to accuse anyone, they stayed away, and some of the eloquent exhibitionists added pride to other faults by supposing that they alone were pious in retaining the prayer meeting.

"But what has this to do with group prayer?" some will ask. "After all, the quotation is from a novel. We are not guilty of that vanity now." Aren't we? I received a candid letter from a friend who accuses herself of this very thing. She has caught herself out. She now realizes that she was guilty of this for years. She is so ashamed that she wants to give all her prayer time now to silent prayer, bidding prayer, read prayer—and most of it in private. She wrote:

> I was too much aware of other people's presence. I played to the gallery, glowed when someone said, "Amen," and tended to choose prayers and petitions which would be pleasing to the hearers. I launched into prayer as others would have burst into song on a concert platform or attempted a brilliant shot on a tennis court: "Watch me! This is it!" I did not find God in this kind of praying. I lost Him in preoccupation with myself and the impression I was making on others.

Exhibitionism isn't an appropriate topic for discussion when the prayer group is meeting. This is for the private discourse of the soul with God. Go someplace in quietness, therefore, and sit unhurried in the presence of the Holy Spirit. Ask Him to search you. For your soul's sake, don't hurry. Just sit exposed to the Uncreated Beam. If conviction of guilt comes, spread your need out before Him and ask Him to burn this exhibitionism out of your soul as by acid.

Avoiding the Dangers

These are some of the perils of prayer; there are many others, for the Evil One strews the path with hindrances, allurements, fears, and snares. The last thing he wants is for a Christian to become mighty in prayer, for such a person can hurl evil from its throne and rescue multitudes from the sleep of death. A wise group leader will be able to guide the members, point out the dangers, and show how the great prayer warriors of the past have triumphed. For lack of such training, many today become disappointed with prayer. They have lost their first love, and faith has died.

I believe that more spiritual casualties occur through forsaking prayer than from any other cause. That is why prayer cells are so important; they are schools where Christians learn to pray, and to pray effectively. Prayer maintains contact with the resources of heaven. When prayer stops, the sustaining vine is severed and it is only a question of time before the soul begins to wither and shrivel. The fruitful branch of Jesus Christ must preserve that connection at all costs. He watches and prays.

Chapter 6

Prayer and the Bible

And search the oracles divine,
Till every heartfelt word be mine.
                    —Charles Wesley

If you want to explore the great ranges of Christian prayer, your mind must be steeped in the Scriptures. You do not need to be a profound scholar nor to have a large library, though a few good commentaries can be very useful. The devotional approach to the Bible is quite different from the critical; the secret lies in the attitude toward it. A supercilious visitor once said to a little girl, "I see you are reading the Bible." "No, sir," she replied, "The Bible is reading me."

Stand humbly and quietly before the Book. Let its great truths soak in. Through the operation of the Holy Spirit, the Bible will search your soul, expose the shams and deceits, reveal the mind of God to you, and bring you to the Cross. Don't be put off by the parts of the Bible you do not understand. Leave them for later. Begin with the parts you do. As Tom Sawyer said, it wasn't the bits he didn't understand that worried him; it was the parts he did.

Because you are using your Bible as an aid to prayer, it is not necessary to read more than a verse or two and then to ponder on their meaning. It is helpful to use a daily devotional book that briefly expounds a passage and concludes with a prayer. As your knowledge of the Scriptures grows, you can move on to the study of a particular book of the Bible. But return often to the Gospels.

In his autobiography, *From Faith to Faith,* W. E. Orchard draws a picture of his devout grandfather that I have long loved.

> What a business he made of his Bible-reading! When he came home from work, after his meal, he shaved, dressed himself more carefully and then settled down to the Bible, set under the lamp on the table before him. When the Book had been opened at the proper place, his spectacles had to be polished to the accompaniment of anticipatory sighs over the treasures he was about to explore. The spectacles then being as carefully adjusted, a verse was slowly read, half aloud to himself. Deeper sighs then followed, perhaps accompanied by the exclamation "This blessed Book!" Further reflections would bring forth joyful tears, which meant that the spectacles had to be wiped again, and so on, but always with the same deliberation.

I suppose some people would brush this aside as bibliolatry, but I can't. The big business of the old man's day was his time with God's Word. What reverence—even in his dress! How he puts himself to school to the book! How obviously he feeds his soul on what he finds! Will anyone write this old man off as a "fundamentalist" (whatever they mean by that blurred word)? Is there something in his attitude that we want to keep (or recover), or has the biblical criticism of the last century taken this reverent approach to the Book from us forever?

I cannot think so. John Wesley's own attitude would be accepted, I think, even outside Methodism as proof of that. What devotion Wesley had to the Holy Book! How he loved to proclaim himself—despite his wide reading—as "a man of one book"! How positive he was that this was, in the most special sense, God's own word. Yet the developing character of the biblical revelation of God was axiomatic with John Wesley. He said flatly that the imprecatory psalms were not fit to be read in public worship. I can never imagine him defending the slaughter of the women and children of the Amalekites the way I heard a Bible student do so: "Well, their menfolk had been killed, so it was probably the kindest thing to slaughter the women and children also. Life would have been difficult for them alone."

Reading With Confidence

We are not driven to these extremes. The Bible, as the supreme book of religion, is there for us to feed on in complete confidence. I cannot think that long arguments about the sun standing still or the possibility of a man living in a whale get us anywhere. I want to come to the Bible in the spirit (if not entirely in the manner) of Dr. Orchard's grandfather: "This blessed Book!" Let me give my whole mind to it. Let me mine there for the richest ore in literature. Let me stay my soul on its dependable promises.

When the coffin is standing by the bed of my dearest, I can't afford to fall to wondering if Christ did or did not say, "In my Father's house are many mansions." I know it's a translation of a translation. But is that the accurate sense of what He said? When the doctor says my illness is terminal, I can't fall to wondering if Christ is a dependable guide through life. I've proved Him so and confirmed the biblical promises through many years. I rest on them now. Come at it rightly, and the Bible will never fail.

But someone may ask, "How do you come at it rightly?" I would say, "You must come to the Word with the special help of the Holy Spirit." The Bible was given by the inspiration of the Holy Spirit; it can only be properly read by the same divine help. He who gave it illuminates it. He who spoke through prophet and apostle knows best how to use what He has given. I am certain that there is a special relationship between the Holy Spirit and the Holy Book. Let me draw that out in connection with prayer.

Unbelievers say sometimes that "you can prove anything from the Bible," and it would be fair of us to admit some point in what they say. If people have a mind to it, polygamy and slavery can both be defended with big names from the Old Testament. There is so much in the Bible that people (especially if they ignore the context and forget to see all things in the light of Christ) can quote it for nearly anything they like. A high authority has told us that the Devil can quote Scripture when it suits him.

How do you decide, in any time of special need, what part of the Bible is relevant to your exact circumstances? Is it this, or that? They may be opposite pieces of counsel. We all know how ordinary proverbs cancel each other out. Is it "Look before you leap," or "He who hesitates is lost"? Do Bible texts run counter to each other in that fashion? How does a person in time of need know which is the special word from the Word? God guides through the Bible and often answers our prayers by it. How do we know "the relevant word"?

This is an office of the Holy Spirit. I testify (as millions more would do) that when we turn to God in need, the Holy Spirit Himself selects the relevant word. In a certain crisis years ago, I was deeply perplexed which of two texts I should apply: "Let not thy left hand know what thy right hand doeth" or "Let your light so shine before men, that they may see your good works, and glorify your Father which is in heaven." On the surface they appeared contradictory. But after unhurried prayer, I had not the slightest doubt which was the relevant word. It was as though the Spirit took the word He wanted and said, "This is it. This one now."

Living in the Word

I believe the Spirit can use other books too. I know what blessing has come to my own soul from the writings of the saints. Yet none of these challenge the uniqueness of the Bible. This is the supreme book. Begotten of God, it is daily used by God. Prayer knits into it in a way that is altogether special. Of other books we say, "That man's thoughts are very helpful." But with the illumination of the Holy Spirit on the Bible we say, "This is the word of God." As we appropriate the truths of the Bible we begin to base our thinking on its standards, to breathe its air. We begin to live in it.

The Bible is unique. It is the only full unfolding of the plan of God for earth. It is the only record of God's dealing with the most spiritually sensitive people of the ancient world. It is the only record of the life of the Son of God on earth. It is the only record of the beginning of the Christian church.

The Bible is effective. It gives meaning to life. It is one of the chief ways by which God speaks to us still. It has fed the souls of millions for many hundreds of years. It has fully sustained people in the fiercest trials known to our race— sorrow, shame, pain, prison, despair, death.

The Bible is timeless. In its central meaning it is never out of date. It speaks eternal truth to every generation in its time. The fiercest criticism leaves its spiritual truth undimmed. We can foresee no time when it will be surpassed.

Yet the Bible isn't all easy to understand. Picking bits at random can be dangerous. Only serious, reverent, and prayerful study secures its treasures. This takes time—and we have crowded our lives with other things. So let us resolve to know this book better, to learn to live in it, to give time to it daily, to wait on the Holy Spirit before we turn a page, to focus our aim on the Word within the word, to let God apply it to the soul, to store our memory with the phrases He selects, to walk in its light until we walk into heaven.

Here is an example of this kind of Bible meditation. First, read Matthew 6:5–6.

And when thou prayest, thou shalt not be as the hypocrites are: for they love to pray standing in the synagogues and in the corners of the streets, that they may be seen of men. Verily I say unto you, They have their reward.

But thou, when thou prayest, enter into thy closet, and when thou hast shut thy door, pray to thy Father which is in secret; and thy Father which seeth in secret shall reward thee openly.

Then muse on it. Jesus is saying that if we really want to know God, we must retire from the public scene and from the business, duties, and pleasures of everyday life to some quiet place where we shall not be disturbed. "And close the door behind you," He says. "Shut out the invading clamor of the street."

> From the world of sin, and noise,
> And hurry I withdraw;
> For the small and inward voice
> I wait with humble awe.

Such withdrawal, Jesus says, is essential. For the Father whom we seek is a hidden God. He lives in secret, He works in secret, and He sees in secret. He is hidden from all, yet nothing is hidden from Him. He cannot be observed or detected by any physical or psychological test. He is never discovered until He reveals Himself. And we must enter the secret place to find Him.

By going into a quiet room or some other secluded spot alone, you direct and adjust your whole being toward God. By going secretly, unknown even to your dearest, you prove your sincere intention to seek Him for Himself. Jesus warns us against the religiosity that wants people to know of its zeal. People like that enjoy praying in public. It is a form of exhibitionism. They are gratified by the observation of the onlookers. That is the reward they want, and that is all they will get. They are not really seeking God, but the acclamation of men.

The true meeting with God is so intensely personal, the self-examination so humiliating, the conversation so confidential and intimate, the dialogue so holy, that it needs a secret place. Remember, God sees the secret places of your soul; nothing can be hidden from Him. Samuel Chadwick warns us that "hearts must be pure and hands clean that dare shut the door and be alone with God."

But the results will be evident to all, for the Father who sees in secret will reward you openly.

Here is another example. Consider James 5:17:

> Elias was a man subject to like passions as we are, and he prayed earnestly that it might not rain: and it rained not on the earth by the space of three years and six months.

Elijah's spectacular achievements as a man of God grip the imagination and seem to be far beyond the capacity of ordinary men. No, says James; Elijah was a man like us, with the same emotions and weaknesses. He was mighty in faith, because he was mighty in prayer: "he prayed earnestly." The margin of the Revised Version (1881) translates this "he prayed in his prayer." The curious Greek is in fact a transliteration rather than a translation of the Hebrew infinitive absolute, a way of emphasizing the action of the verb. It means he prayed intensely.

As Samuel Chadwick noted, Elijah did not merely *say* his prayers; he really *prayed* his prayers. The intensity of his beseeching made them effective. He knew God could do what he wanted. He knew it ought to be done to save the soul of his people. He was willing to become part of the strategy of heaven, cost what it may. So James says, "Very potent is the effective petition of a righteous man."

When we have felt God's will in prayer and are ready to make His will ours—to identify ourselves with His purposes—then our pleadings are irresistible. We are asking in the name and Spirit of Jesus—and as He promised, whatever we ask in His name, God will do it for us.

Exploring the Scriptures

The Bible thus used is the great handbook on prayer. It would be a most fruitful enterprise for the prayer cell to study the Bible references to prayer one after another. You could begin, for instance, with what Jesus has to say about prayer. Note the times He prayed, the places He chose for this communion with God, the things He prayed about, and the guidance and instruction He gave to His disciples. Perhaps one member could summarize the thoughts and comments of the group. If these ideas were written up after each session, you could compile a little devotional commentary for use by your members and friends, for it is wise to treasure up the insights you have received.

Such exploring of the Scriptures, however, should be kept within strict limits. It is a preparation for prayer, not a substitute. The cell is not a study circle. The passage can be followed up by further study at home. The purpose of the exposition is to deepen our understanding of prayer and help us to pray more effectively by filling our minds with biblical truth. Through such meditation the Holy Spirit illumines the Bible and makes us receptive to its message. Wesley, as usual, has a verse for it:

> Come, divine Interpreter,
> Bring us eyes Thy Book to read,
> Ears the mystic words to hear,
> Words which did from Thee proceed,
> Words that endless bliss impart,
> Kept in an obedient heart.

Chapter 7

The Lord's Prayer

I am prepared to believe in good news direct from my God. I am prepared to believe in the most marvelous Divine Sympathy with my condition, because I believe the Infinite God is my Father. —John Pulsford

It was after they had been watching the Master at prayer that one of the disciples, on behalf of them all, said, "Lord, teach us to pray" (Luke 11:1). If they realized their need to be taught, surely we ought not to spurn instruction. Are not we too scholars in the school of Christ?

The disciples were men of prayer. They were devout Jews who had been taught to pray at their father's knee. They knew the prayers of the home, the psalms, and the majestic liturgies of the synagogue and the temple. But as they watched Jesus at prayer, as they began to understand what prayer meant to Him and what it did for Him, they realized that they knew scarcely anything about the *power* of prayer. That is why they asked to be taught the secret of praying as Jesus prayed. And the Lord immediately and gladly complied with their request. "This is the way to pray," He said, and He taught them the Lord's Prayer.

Throughout the world, Christians of every creed repeat His prayer. But merely to say these words as if they were some kind of magical formula is to miss their whole significance. Do you really *know* the Lord's Prayer? It is the great model prayer, each little phrase summarizing an essential element of comprehensive prayer. We only begin to understand it when we realize that it is a kind of prescription of the ingredients of prayer. We must set ourselves seriously to the lifelong study of the Lord's Prayer, taking it very slowly, phrase by phrase, each day probing more deeply into the significance of each sentence.

Contemplating God

The first three clauses of the Lord's Prayer are directed toward the contemplation of God. We do not start with our wants and petitions; we look at God and think about Him. God is in the center of our thoughts, not us.

"Our Father"

We begin with our Father. I read a tribute to a retired pastor in which the writer said, "I shall never forget his sermon on the Lord's Prayer. He said he had begun to study it twenty-six years ago and was still exploring the glories hidden in 'Our Father.'"

If God is our Father, then I am a brother to every man on earth. No distinction of class or race, creed or color, must be allowed to destroy that essential unity. I am committed to the classless, multiracial society of the kingdom of heaven.

But if God is my Father, then who am I? No longer an insignificant particle of matter on a tiny planet on the outskirts of the galaxy. I am the heir of heaven, my Father's child. A new poise, a new dignity is mine compared with which the distinctions of earth, the medals, the ranking, the titles, and all the social gradings of this world are ephemeral.

Billy Bray, a famous Cornish preacher of the nineteenth century, was once accosted by a hard-sweating squire who upbraided him in the foulest language. Billy bore the tirade in silence and then asked quietly, "Sir, is that a fitting way to address a king's son?"

"A king's son?" repeated the amazed squire. "You're Billy Bray, aren't you?"

"Yes, sir, I am Billy Bray. And my Father is a great King."

As we dwell on the fatherhood of God we begin to grasp the wonder of it. A new note steals into our voice, a strange joy fills the heart.

The disciples, who often heard Jesus pray, could never forget how He pronounced the word *Father*. "Abba," He said in His native Aramaic. They tried to say it like Him, with the same caress in it, the same reverential awe. They talked of it after He had ascended. They told Paul what it sounded like. Paul caught the lilt and glory of it and urged his friends, the sons of God, to say "Abba, Father" like Jesus Himself.

"Which art in heaven"

It is easy to be shortsighted in prayer. We can only see the four walls of the little room. But though the space is small, God is not little. Even if the walls were transparent and we could see to the ends of the earth, the span of our thought could not measure the greatness of God. The Lord's Prayer is prayed against the background of heaven. We look beyond the far-flung galaxies of space; we leap beyond the chasms of time, seeking the center and source of all creation. Prayer breaks through into dimensions unlimited by space and time. We address our Father, who is in heaven.

What is heaven? Some theologians have said, "Heaven is not a place; it is a condition." This is true in the sense that you cannot reach heaven by traveling through space, but it leaves the earthbound mind with the false impression that heaven is nowhere. The truth could perhaps be better stated by saying that "there are forms of space that can only be experienced under certain spiritual conditions. The dead soul cannot reach heaven, the redeemed soul can." Heaven is the home of God. It is the level of existence wherein those who love Him see Him and serve Him.

Our earthbound minds can only use symbols to describe heaven. We picture it as the glorious throne from which the entire universe is controlled. It blazes with uncreated light. Before it stand the great spirits who perfectly obey God's will, yet even they, who have never known sin, veil their faces before the awful majesty of Him who sits upon the throne. And around the throne stand the hosts of the redeemed, for they have access to the Presence through Jesus Christ, who shares the throne.

It was Jesus who taught us to call God "Father." He revealed the Father's love and hunger for wayward man. But Jesus insistently guards the glorious name from the abuses of crude familiarity and superficiality. Awe and worship blend with love as we look into the heavenly places. Nature can teach us little about heaven, and even grace can only point the way. Heaven and even the Heaven of Heavens cannot contain God. He fills all heaven, but heaven does not confine Him.

True worship silences even the praises of heaven. An old minister was once called upon to fill in at the last moment for a famous, golden-tongued preacher. The packed congregation murmured in audible disappointment as the white-haired figure climbed slowly into the pulpit. But as he announced his first hymn, the awe and adoration in the trembling voice instantly deflected all attention from himself to the God they had come to worship. In the deep hush, the presence of God filled the place and the people knew that the old saint had opened the door of heaven for them. He read,

> God is a name my soul adores.
> The almighty Three, the eternal One;
> Nature and grace, with all their powers,
> Confess the Infinite unknown.

And yet this unknown Infinite cares for the children of men and from that throne of glory has sent the Beloved to visit and redeem us. Through the blood of Christ there is now a way for us to rise to that sublime abode; we can now approach the eternal throne in confidence.

Heaven is our Father's house. It contains many dwelling places, great star cities of the hosts of heaven. It is our true home, the goal of our pilgrimage, and every day brings us that much nearer to the moment when we shall see Him as He is and shall be with Him always. And so we pray, "Our Father which art in heaven."

"Hallowed be thy name"

Our modern age has little idea of what "hallowed" means. The word is strange, as one schoolteacher found who asked her students to write out the Lord's Prayer. "Alfred by Thy name," wrote one, and another puzzled child wrote, "Hollow head be the name."

Hallowed. "Let it be made holy or sacred"—that is what it means. But God is holy. His name is holy. How can anyone or anything make His name holy? What did Jesus mean by this strange command, the first petition of this prayer?

The thought of Jesus was steeped in the Old Testament. He fed His soul on its rich nourishment. The prophecy of Malachi has a passage that these opening words of the Lord's Prayer seem to summarize. Here, within the narrow framework of Jewish nationalism, the ideas of the fatherhood of God and His essential holiness are brought together. Malachi asks,

> Have we not all one father? hath not one God created us? why do we deal treacherously every man against his brother, by profaning the covenant of our fathers?
>
> Judah hath dealt treacherously, and an abomination is committed in Israel and in Jerusalem; for Judah hath profaned the holiness of the LORD which he loved (2:10−11).

Because God is the Father of us all, we are brethren; we ought therefore to help and love one another, not hate and destroy one another. In our refusal to act as brothers, we are breaking the great covenant that binds men to God and therefore to each other. Such action is a desecration of the pure and holy relationship that ought to exist between man and God and consequently between man and man. Evil profanes the Holy Society. The prophet denounces his people because they have profaned the holiness of the Lord, whom once they loved, by giving themselves to false gods. Man always does. Unless he keeps himself faithful to the only true God, he falls under the spell of seductive imagery that will destroy him.

Jesus takes this truth and states it, not as a terrible negative warning, but as a positive and joyous command. He does not say, "Do not profane the holiness of God"; He says, "Hallowed be thy name." Let us in all our actions reveal the holiness of God.

And how do we do that? By letting the holy love of God possess us, by seeking the mind of Christ so that—thinking like Him, feeling as He feels, and doing what He wants us to do—our own hearts will become a copy of the loving heart of Jesus. Charles Wesley truly reads the significance of the phrase when he prays,

> That I Thy mercy may proclaim,
> That all mankind Thy truth may see,
> Hallow Thy great and glorious name,
> And perfect holiness in me.

There are two sides to holiness, a mystical and an ethical. The two must come together in Christian holiness or "perfect love" or "entire sanctification"—call it what you will. One side is expressed by saying that there is a divine quality about the holy life that is indefinable and indescribable, but nonetheless real, for it bears the mark of God upon it; it shines with its own radiance. The other side is expressed by saying that the holy life is also one of consistent goodness. Sin destroys the holiness, which departs and vanishes, for God will not share His nature with evil. The truly holy heart is the truly loving heart, the heart that loves as Christ loves.

When these two aspects are kept together we avoid that repulsive parody of holiness—the self-righteous, censorious, and bigoted spirit that has so often brought "holiness" into disrepute. People begin to understand the name of God when His nature begins to shine through what we are.

One of the most beautiful musical settings of the Lord's Prayer is a West Indian one in which the phrase "Hallowed be thy name" is used as a chorus after each petition of the prayer, riveting each thought into the holy name of God. Let us look more closely at the name.

The thought of Jesus concentrates on God himself. Only Jesus knew the full meaning of the name of God. He invites us to contemplate the wonder of that name. Think of the holy names disclosed in the Scriptures. Consider God's revelation of Himself to Moses and the wonderful title "I AM THAT I AM." This means that God is a person, not a thing; He is Someone, not something. Only persons can know Him. He calls us to the heights of full personal life.

In ancient thought, a name is never just a label, still less just a sound; it is the essence of the thing itself, the real definition of the person to whom it belongs. We know some of the names of God, but one day we shall learn—if we have been faithful—the great name, for Jesus has promised, "I will write upon him the name of my God, . . . and I will write upon him my new name" (Rev. 3:12). That is the name that completely sums up the nature and essence of God.

> Write Thy new name upon my heart,
> Thy new, best name of love

If we truly know the nature of Jesus—that is, understand who He is and what He has done and is doing—if we know His purpose and have caught the significance of His life, death, and resurrection, then His name is becoming known to us. And if we are willing to become His disciples, to learn of Him and imitate Him, so that we begin to think and act like Him, then His power and the resources of His heavenly kingdom are at our disposal.

This is the basis of the Lord's repeated injunction that whatever we ask in His name, the Father will do for us. Of course He will! For then we are Christ's and Christ is God's. The Father delights to continue His work through us.

> Thy name to me, Thy nature grant;
> This, only this be given:
> Nothing beside my God I want,
> Nothing in earth or heaven.

"Thy kingdom come"

For many ancient peoples the golden age was in the past; they pined for a primitive innocence when there was no sin or sorrow, no disease or death, when age did not destroy the beauty of youth and no strife marred the peaceful years.

The Jews too had their legends of this harmonious age. They placed it at the very beginning of the human story, and they went on to tell how man by his disobedience to the holy will lost Paradise and was expelled from that lovely garden of innocent beauty. Yet in the very moment of his shame and exile, a hope was given him that someday a son of man would find the way back and bring a redeemed humanity once more into a paradise regained.

Through the long centuries of exile the hope grew, in spite of the suffering, the sin, and the rebellion of the proud spirit of man. Spiritual giants outlined the picture ever more clearly, pointing to the coming of this Messiah. Their disappointments drove them closer to God, and in the anguish of their souls they learned some of the secrets of the coming kingdom.

They saw the kingdoms of man, the pomp and pageantry, the lust for power, the rule of might, the overweening pride, and they began to long for another kingdom—the kingdom of God—based not on pride but humility, a kingdom whose power was commanded by love. They saw the tragic procession of empires—Egypt, Assyria, Babylon, Greece, and Rome—rising and falling, and they yearned for the everlasting kingdom whose eternal order and harmony could be seen in the silent procession of the countless stars by night and in the annual sequence of the seasons. They longed for a divine community where God Himself would wipe away each tear, where sorrow and sighing would flee away, where there would be no more death.

This is the vision of the kingdom of God that has haunted all prophets and seers, that lurks in all our finest poetry and music, that rises from the very depths of man's heart. For man is an exile and he longs for home.

But he longs not just for the relief this kingdom will bring to man's burdened spirit. It is our Father's kingdom. He is the great King. The kingdom expresses His nature and His will; it reflects His character. The greatest delight is the vision of the King Himself.

> The King there, in His beauty,
> Without a veil is seen;
> It were a well-spent journey,
> Though seven deaths lay between.

Though we must wait for the trumpet call before we see the full glories of that kingdom, we can in some measure enter it now and see it in action here among the dark kingdoms of men. The same peace that fills the shining courts of heaven can fill our hearts as we give a cup of cold water in His name, for then the kingdom of heaven is in us.

"Thy kingdom come," then, means both a heartfelt plea

for the consummation of the ages and an equally heartfelt longing that the kingdom will express itself in and through us in all our daily living.

"Thy will be done in earth, as it is in heaven"

In some old hymnals there was a section entitled "Resignation—For Believers Suffering," and several of the hymns in this group ended with the words "Thy will be done." The dominant theme of the section was to encourage afflicted Christians to bear their burdens without complaint and to trust the inscrutable but always wise and loving will of God, even when that will stripped them of comfort, took from them their loved ones, subjected them to the ravages of disease, or allowed them to be persecuted. Believers must learn to forgo their own likes and preferences and to submit their will to the will of God.

Now there is much truth in all this. There are times when the will of God seems to bear down heavily upon us and confronts us with a path of suffering and sorrow that we would give much to avoid. There are times when the will of God asks of us some costly sacrifice that we are not always willing to make. In the struggle we come to our little Gethsemane and have to say, "Father, let this cup pass from me; nevertheless, not my will but Thine be done." But the Gethsemane experience is a very special application of the rule and indeed presupposes a lifetime of joyful and willing acceptance of God's will.

In the Lord's Prayer the theme is not one of resignation at all, but of fervent intercession. The prayer is a plea that earth may become again part of the domain of heaven, with all the peace, glory, and joy of the heavenly kingdom.

How do you picture heaven? Do you see it as a present reality, a realm in which vast populations of intelligent creatures—not all of human stock by any means—live in a community of perfect contentment and harmony? Many folk, when they think of space, imagine it peopled with horribly inhuman monsters who would destroy the earth if they could find their way there. They forget that we have already had one invasion from outer space. One inhabitant of another world came here; His name was Jesus. He came from the glory of the Father, and He came not to destroy, but to save. He came to restore us to the community of the heavenly kingdom.

In this prayer, Jesus is longing for the peace of His home and yearning for earth to share it. Thus He tells us to pray, "Thy kingdom come. Thy will be done in earth, as it is in heaven." There the Father's will is done gladly and freely by all. God's will is their peace and joy. God's wisdom directs their every move. They live ever sensitive and obedient to what God wants them to do. Jesus wants us and all mankind to live like that.

That is not resignation, but self-realization. That is not submission, but fulfillment. It brings heaven to earth and makes earth part of heaven.

Concerning Mankind

As the first three clauses of the Lord's Prayer are directed to the contemplation of God, the next three concern man. Having placed ourselves within the will of God, we turn our attention to man and his needs.

"Give us this day our daily bread"

Here, right in the middle of the Lord's Prayer, comes the stark realism that recognizes our physical needs and sees them to be just as much part of the divine providence as our most spiritual desires.

Christianity is the great reconciler. Body and soul are a unity, and each needs the other. The temptation to separate the material from the spiritual is a fatal error that leads to the abuse of both. A religion that does not recognize the needs of man's physical nature becomes lopsided and unhealthy, and a materialism that ignores the spiritual becomes blind and deadening. Christianity truly understood is the most material of all religions.

The body needs food and it needs it every day. Two thousand years ago many used to starve to death for lack of food; flood and drought could bring unrelieved disaster. Nowadays we carry vast surpluses which can tide us over bad harvests, and modern fertilizers and selective breeding have greatly increased the quality and quantity of food production. But still food is essentially the annual gift of God. Man toils, but God gives the increase. Without Him and the ordered universe He has made, there would be no harvest, no grain to sow, no miracle of generation.

Since, then, all heaven and all earth belong to God, and we have nothing apart from Him, we remember our utter and complete dependence on His grace and faithfulness. Daily we depend on the Giver, and we are facing reality when we recognize that we live because of His continual care. This is the sober truth, and those who take the food of the earth for granted, or imagine that they feed themselves, are deceiving themselves. That is why the daily prayer for bread should be complemented by the grace at meals, the act of thanksgiving for the answered prayer. "And Jesus took bread, and when He had given thanks . . ."

Then we begin to think of a hungry world and the appalling maldistribution that leaves three-quarters of mankind with so little. Can we rest at ease when other children of our Father have not enough to eat? What are we doing with the resources of power and wealth at our disposal? We are launched on the economics of the kingdom. No man who has ever truly prayed the Lord's Prayer can shut his ears to the cry of the hungry children of the world, the refugees, the people of the undeveloped countries.

Man does not live by bread alone, but neither can we live

without it. We who need the Bread of Heaven need also the bread of earth.

The two are not so separate as some people think. The one is a picture of the other. Jesus once took a loaf of earthly bread, and having given thanks, He broke it and gave it to His disciples, saying, "This is my body, which is broken for you." Those who eat that bread have meat indeed. It feeds both body and soul. To the man of faith, every earthly meal becomes a blessed sacrament of Holy Communion, and the Lord's Supper becomes a feast indeed.

"And forgive us our debts, as we forgive our debtors"

We come next to that part of the Lord's Prayer that describes an element of the discipline of every day. We may be able to concentrate on only one other phrase of the prayer in any discussion, but this transaction must never be omitted or we will defeat the whole purpose of the prayer.

As we place ourselves before God and expose ourselves to His Spirit, we become increasingly conscious of the blemishes in our character, our failure to grasp and do His will. From time to time He shows us things that are wrong that we never dreamed existed. The moments of hot shame, as we remember what we have done, are agonizing. We turn to God again and ask Him to forgive and to expunge.

God will and does. He has promised that if we truly and earnestly repent and confess, He will surely forgive us and cleanse us from all unrighteousness (1 John 1:9). But only on one condition: that we ourselves forgive, that we let go of the hurt and resentment we entertain against anyone else. If we do not forgive, we cannot be forgiven (Matt. 6:15). A man who refuses to forgive destroys the bridge he himself must cross.

Some people nurse a resentment for years. They do not realize that every time they say the Lord's Prayer it becomes a bitter blasphemy, searing and shriveling their souls. He who refuses to forgive commits spiritual suicide, for he destroys himself. He has severed the spiritual artery by which the life of God flows into the soul. We cannot afford to harbor resentment, anger, jealousy, ill-feeling, and hate. Forgiveness is the only way to get these poisons out of the system. God can do no mighty work in the soul until we open our hearts and let go our sense of injury. So ask yourself bluntly, Have I done much forgiving lately? It is a hard, costly business; painful and unpleasant, too.

First somebody upsets you—a slight, an unkind criticism, an unjust aspersion. Some people with whom you work seem to glory in finding fault with you. How they gloat if they can show you have forgotten something or not done something! How they love to put you in the wrong! They seem to be waiting for you to make a mistake, waiting to pounce and make you feel small. You can see the satisfaction in their small, tight lips, the gleam of triumph they cannot keep out of their eyes.

These pinpricks are harder to bear than major disasters. We can at times rise to the great challenge, but a long-drawn-out series of petty persecutions or provocations can speedily induce resentment and bitterness. It is easy to be lovable to those who like us. It is extremely difficult to be lovable to those who dislike us. After all, we are only human. It hurts to be criticized, humiliated, rebuked, or ignored.

What can we do about it? The saints have always known that to cope with the petty irritation is one of the major battles of holiness. The royal road to success is to get ourselves into a frame of mind that can take this form of trial and use it to God's glory.

Brother Lawrence encountered hurt in his kitchen, where the mean-spirited monks, jealous of his sanctity, made his life a misery. They found imaginary spots on his pans and made him wash them again; they spilled things on the floor and made him scrub it again; they indulged in a campaign to humiliate and break him.

Lawrence prayed for his fellow monks, not complainingly, but thanking God for them. He saw them as instruments of God's will who were sent to purify his spirit and cleanse it of all self and pride. He was certain God would not allow anything really harmful to befall him; therefore he believed that this apparent persecution must come with God's permission, if not His will. If that was so, he could bring great gain if rightly used. So he poured himself into the extra work, the shame, and the humiliation and offered not resentment, but love. In the end those who had so ill-used him realized they were not fit to touch his sandals. But he thought of them as friends, messengers from God who were helping to discipline his spirit.

If we gain this poise of spirit, then we can begin to handle the situation. First we refrain from passing swift judgment on those who hurt us. We hold the proud self in check while we ask ourselves a few questions: Are we so sure we are right? may there not be considerable fault in us which our critics have seen and to which we ourselves are blind? The way they point it out may be unpleasant and hurtful, but if we can correct the fault, if we can eradicate this blemish from our character, then we ought to thank them; they are really helping us.

If we are absolutely certain that we are blameless and have been wrongly accused, then the second line of defense is to remember that we are responsible only for the way we act, not for others' behavior. How we react will show what kind of disciple we really are. Our restraint, grace, humility, and refusal to become angry, to quarrel, or to defend ourselves may at first exacerbate the hostility, for it carries its own rebuke; but in the end it will win the real victory.

So we must learn to forgive. When we stop forgiving we stop growing and begin to shrivel in spirit. It will cost many tears, many secret heartbreaks, and many struggles, but it brings rich rewards. Not least is the comfort and peace of the Holy Spirit that fills the soul when we have let the resentment go. But even more wonderful is the forgiveness that God lets flow toward us. He pours on us the transforming energy that fits us for the life of His eternal kingdom. Compared with such a prize, how small is the cost of our forgiving love!

The determination to keep resentment out of the soul must become the ruling passion of our prayer life until, like the Lord Himself, our response to the most terrible assault can be "Father, forgive them." That is the goal. How paltry are our little grievances compared with the wounds of the Man of Sorrows! And if we are prepared to sacrifice our resentments and ask God to help us to forgive, how rich is the reward! Then His own forgiving grace will flood through these newly opened channels of the soul.

One of the most striking characteristics of the Welsh Revival of 1904–6 was the melting of hearts in the great prayer meetings. In the crowded churches where people were coming and going all day long, there was continual reconciliation of estranged friends. While prayer was being offered, people would get up from their seats to beg forgiveness of their neighbors for things said and done. This was bound to happen, for God was moving among them and they, seeking His forgiveness, had to forgive each other. Then the blessing poured out from heaven.

I can think of no more urgent business for prayer cells than for people to take the Lord's Prayer seriously and to spend a session facing the business of forgiveness. What doors this would unlock! What powers it would release!

"Lead us not into temptation"

There used to be a railway stop in London called Thames Station. Once a little fellow asked his father, "Why does the

Bible say, 'Lead us not into Thames Station,' Dad? What's wrong with it?" The little boy is not the only one who has been puzzled by this phrase in the Lord's Prayer.

James says bluntly that God tempts nobody (James 1:13). How then can God possibly lead us into temptation?

There is real difficulty here, and I am not happy with the suggestion that there has been a mistranslation of the original Aramaic word that means both "to undergo" and "to go under." This assumes that what Jesus actually said was "Do not let us go under in temptation" and that the Gospel writers did not know enough Greek to avoid the serious blunder of selecting the wrong verb.

I prefer to think that we have an accurate translation of what the Lord said and that we must face the difficulty, not evade it. We get almost the same words in Matthew 4:1: "Then was Jesus led up of the Spirit into the wilderness to be tempted of the devil." Jesus went into that dreadful ordeal under the strong compulsion of the Holy Spirit. There is a dark mystery here. Faith knows that God tempts no man, that He is implacably opposed to evil. Yet He controls all things, even the time and place of evil. A similar experience occurred in Gethsemane. Christ prayed hard for the cup of suffering to be removed, but God still pressed it on Him. Was the Lord saying to His disciples, "Pray that you do not have to go through experiences like that"?

Part of the difficulty is cleared up when we understand what Jesus actually said. "Temptation" is not a complete translation. What Jesus said was, "Do not bring us to the test" (Luke 11:4 NEB). It is not a question of seducing us, but of sorting us out to see what we are really made of. Periods of testing will surely come. The point is, don't go looking for them. To venture before you are ready is to court disaster and expose your inner weakness.

A wise schoolteacher does not schedule stiff examinations before the students are ready. He prepares them thoroughly, not only for the test that is coming, but for the one after that, so that they can take the hurdles in their stride. We are students in the school of Christ, not graduates yet by any means. To go ill-equipped to the test ends, as it did with poor Peter, in the collapse of faith before the onslaught of the world. What an occasion of stumbling it is when a Christian falls and denies his Lord! So let us pray earnestly that God will delay any testing until we are ready for it.

And let us remember that we ourselves will never know when we are really ready. It is just when we think we are strong, Paul reminded us, that we need most to be on our guard. When we are cocksure, we are most likely to come a cropper. Far better the humble heart. When we are aware of our weaknesses and throw ourselves constantly back on God, then we shall survive the tests when they come; for God's strength is made perfect in weakness, and when we are weak, then indeed we are really strong.

So don't go looking for trouble. The adversary is subtle and searches out every weakness of the soul. Put on the whole armor of God and train resolutely for the battle, so that when the day comes we may stand fast.

"Deliver us from evil"

The origins of the English word *evil* are obscure. It may come from a word for "excessive, beyond the tolerable." The general idea, however, is fairly clear. It means something bad, harmful, injurious, malicious, cruel, malignant, painful, disastrous, and destructive. But there are two kinds of evil, and it is important to mark the distinction.

First there is natural evil such as an earthquake that topples a cathedral, as one did in Ecuador some years ago, burying scores of little children who had gone to say their prayers; or a flood that sweeps away a village, destroying men and cattle; or a famine or pestilence that kills tens of thousands.

We call such events "evil" because they destroy human life and happiness and the labor of years. But if these catastrophes had happened in an empty planet, we should not call them evil. They are evil only because of their harmful effects on living, sentient beings. They are evil only because some living person or creature suffers as a result.

We live in a dangerous world where such things can and do happen, and prayer is no guarantee that they will not harm us. God does not suspend the normal working of the universe as a favor or reward to the believer. He makes His sun to shine on the evil and the good, and His rain to fall on the just and the unjust (Matt. 5:45). God will not send a shower for your land because you are a good man while He lets the drought wither the fields of the bad man on the next farm. Prayer is not magic, nor are the answers to prayer favoritism.

So do not imagine that when you pray, "Deliver us from evil," you are gaining immunity from the disasters, plagues, or ills that fall on other people. You won't, and it shows little understanding of the solidarity of humanity to expect preferential treatment from God. He is not that kind of God, and He has not made this world that way.

This is not to say He does not answer prayer. He does, and there are times when such answers appear to be absolute miracles. He is our Father, and there are many occasions when He wonderfully clears the way and diverts disaster from us. But there are also many occasions when He doesn't, but gives us the strength and courage to bear the affliction and suffering. Faith still holds fast to Him, even though it cannot know His reasons.

But there is a second form of evil, and that is moral evil—the perverted mind, the twisted spirit, the sinful heart, the proud, selfish, arrogant, ruthless will that rebels against God and uses other people as if they were things. Thus it enslaves man and cuts him off from God.

This moral evil is always personal; it is evil wrought by someone. It is unfashionable now to believe in a personal devil, though some thinkers are beginning to suspect that there may well be demonic forces that delight in the seduction and possession of human nature. But the evil of one person seems to find an ally in the evil of others, and mass evil seems to have some kind of group mind—a sick, tortured thing that delights in infecting others with its own malignancy.

What Jesus really prayed was "Deliver us from the Evil One." Without developing here any doctrine of the devil, I suggest that we should constantly pray that the spreading cancer of moral evil should find no lodging in our souls.

Behind this simple prayer lies the sharp recognition that such evil surrounds us and is ceaselessly at work trying to enmesh us. He who tries to climb the mount of God will come to know how subtle, how deadly, how persistent are the attacks he has to ward off. It is natural for him to construe his experience as a battle with an unsleeping enemy, a clever, cruel adversary whose one desire is to wrest him away from God and drag him down into the mire and filth of sin. This is a struggle from which there is no respite until the Master calls us from the field of battle. And so our daily prayer must be "Deliver us from the Evil One."

"For thine is the kingdom, and the power, and the glory, for ever"

Observe that none of the earliest manuscripts of the Gospels have this doxology. It was added by the early church in sheer exultation and praise. And if *you* have begun to glimpse the riches of the Lord's Prayer, your soul will be so thankful, so filled with wonder and love, that you cannot refrain from blessing God.

The prayer shows us God's kingdom. It reveals to us the Father's matchless power. It discloses His majesty and glory.

It sets our hearts singing, and we know the song will go on forever. This is the secret joy that preserves the Christian in all the changing scenes of life. He knows the kingdom is there and that finally all will have to recognize its dominion. He knows the power is there, all the energy of the entire universe and the infinite might of God. He has caught a flashing gleam of glory, so wonderful that man's intellect cannot conceive it. All this he has seen in the face of Jesus, who loved him and gave Himself for him. So he goes on his pilgrim way rejoicing and daily blessing the Lord who taught him how to pray.

Chapter 8

Prayer and the Church

If you have Christ in your heart, you are a missionary. If you do not have Christ in your heart, you are a field for missions. —Filomena Natividad
First Methodist Missionary to Okinawa

The essence of prayer is fellowship with God; it is talking to, listening to, and loving the Supreme Being who made and maintains the universe. That such fellowship is possible is so amazing, it ought not to surprise us that some people find it incredible. We would find it incredible ourselves had not long practice and experience left us in no doubt that through prayer we are in contact with the great Other.

Prayer at its best opens earth to heaven. It is the chief means by which the Savior's own prayer can be fulfilled: "Thy will be done in earth, as it is in heaven." If this earth were wide open to heaven by prayer and if we were obedient to godly guidance, earth would be transformed. War would cease; so would race and class hatred, terrorism, hunger, disease. . . .

Some people doubt this. "If prayer is so mighty," they ask, "why hasn't it been the means of more change than has appeared until now? After all, a lot of prayer has been offered through the centuries, yet we still live under the threat of war, with selfishness and hate rampant, with hunger and disease spread wide across the world."

The answer to this is threefold:

—There hasn't been enough prayer.
—The prayer has often been of poor quality.
—We have not been obedient to God's guidance when it came.

Grateful as we are for all the praying souls of the centuries (from whom we have learned so much ourselves), will anyone say that the quality and volume of prayer is worthy of our professed faith or equal to the world's need?

Much of our prayer is selfish. It is "Gimme . . . Gimme . . . Gimme." We are little better than the boy who told the minister he didn't pray every night because there were some nights when he didn't want anything. So much of our prayer is coldly dutiful. It is better than no prayer at all, of course. But prayer without love has no suction; it doesn't draw the blessing down. The sick are not healed or sustained in their serenity. God is not truly adored. Our neighbors are not blessed. We can't say prayer has failed if it has only been of that quality. Such prayer isn't the real thing. Some of us have to learn something we have mistakenly supposed we have understood all our lives.

Don't let this reality depress an earnest beginner. We feel like beginners ourselves. But we mean to go on. If this is the open and neglected secret, we will concentrate on this until we know. No doubt we will die still learning, for only heaven will fully reveal the wonder and rapture of prayer.

What Does the Church Need Most?

Let us test our conviction by asking what it is that the church needs most in this time of her weakness. I tested it myself by asking three intelligent men what they thought the church most needed.

One said, "Better organization." Well, organization is

important, but I honestly think we are reasonably well-organized—though sometimes I wonder if we are organized toward the best goals. How could we be sure of that? Prayer would reveal it.

Another said, "Better preaching." Well, I believe in preaching. I've given years to its study and practice. But what a difference there is between a homiletically sound sermon and a sermon that is both homiletically sound and steeped in prayer from its inception to its delivery.

The third man said, "A higher quality of life in the average Christian." There's a lot in that too. But how does it come except by prayer? I have studied the lives of the saints for half my lifetime and I know no instance of sanctity that did not come out of deep prayer.

Prayer is our great need. All others are dependent on it. We can neglect it if we choose to, but we cannot say that we do not know.

People who work in interdenominational settings sometimes say that Methodism is the most highly organized church in Protestantism. They may be right. With our huge committees, centralized funds, connectional stationing of ministers, and controlling General Conference, it is hard to imagine how any church can be more organized than this.

Organization requires administrators. Having lived close to our administrators for twenty years, I feel free to say that it is hard to imagine also how any church could be better served. Knowing what burdens some of these men carry and how little they see of their homes, I am sure they both need and deserve our prayers. There is no doubt in my mind that we are well served by our administrators.

If administration could bring revival, we would have had it years ago. If keeping the great machine running smoothly and the cash carefully counted could turn our steadily decreasing membership into a swiftly accelerating gain, it would have been done. But it can't. Administration is not inspiration. It is very important in its subordinate place. In its absence, things would soon become chaotic. Yet one mustn't ask what it cannot give.

A subway train is in its way a fine piece of engineering, but it can't move without power, and if it can't move, it can't get the people home. So many people in our country today are "far from home." The church, which would willingly take them, lacks power, and the power is not of human manufacture. How can we get the power? We have an excellent piece of administrative machinery and first-class engineers—but the power? Whence comes it?

The power clearly comes from God, and He is more eager to give it than we are to receive. It does not depend on remote committees. All of us can and should recognize our own duty and privilege to receive. We need to be filled with the love that is the life of God. It can't be "administered" into us; it comes in through adoration. Above all, we need to recover all the range and wonder of intimate dialogue with heaven in prayer. Our administrators are doing all they can do. The inspiration—for lack of which we are in danger of dying—comes this other way.

On one occasion I found Dr. Scott Lidgett, a colleague in the Senate of the University of London, in a rather peevish mood. He remarked tartly on the current criticism of the leaders of the church which was then going around. The people whose church "work" appeared to be to comment adversely on the men whom they had themselves shared in choosing were saying at the time, "Why don't you give us direction?"

"What do they mean?" the old veteran asked me. "Sometimes they complain at the direction we give them. Now they complain because we don't give them enough. Don't they know what the church is for and where we are seeking to go? What do they mean, 'Give us direction'?"

I felt some sympathy with the old man. It may have been

an excess of assurance on my part, but I knew what the church was for and where we were seeking to go. The church (I would have told anyone who asked me) is (1) for the worship of God, (2) for making good men and women, and (3) for Christianizing the social order. I didn't wait for a presidential pronouncement to learn that. "Let's get on with it" seemed to me to be the plain business of every week.

What do these people mean who ask for direction? Do they want another program from denominational headquarters? I think we've had too many. No one knows what response is made to them, and programs that are not followed only bring our leadership into disrespect, and ultimately what happens in the church depends (under God) on plain people like ourselves. It is for us to do what needs to be done in sufficient numbers and with sufficient seriousness, and the miracle will happen. The church will throb and thrill with new life.

Ordinary people like us often underestimate our power. Even in a highly authoritative church like the Roman Communion, it is the ordinary people who do things. No one who knows the history of Lourdes can doubt that the hierarchy hindered it and the ordinary people insisted on it. Is leadership from the top or the bottom? In the church of God, I believe, the people can have (under divine guidance) what they want. They don't have to wait for a man in office or in robes to tell them what to want. Let them go in little groups to the God who loves to lead them, and they will know what to do in their local situation. The multiplication of that knowledge and obedience will transform the national situation too. It is up to us—under God. It is His direction we need, and we can have it for the asking.

It is against this background that prayer groups are needed. People who still look on prayer meetings snobbishly as an occupation for a few old-fashioned "fundies" had better think again. In home, church, neighborhood, and the workplace, the prayer cell can be the big business of every week. It opens earth to heaven. It solves problems, directs energies, lifts burdens, and makes God real. It is for us plain folk to get on with it, sustaining our present cells and forming or inspiring others. The Holy Spirit is working, and there is no limit to what He can do. It is God who leads us. We have only to follow and obey.

What Is a "Successful" Church?

Does the phrase "a successful church" sound strange and ironic to you? Well, think of it as the kind of church Jesus would want, and then you can begin.

If you were to ask a group of Christians, "What is a successful church?" you would probably receive a variety of answers. Some would say, "A crowded church," but every devout preacher knows that a crowd is only an opportunity, not an achievement. Some would say, "Any church where the sacrament of Holy Communion is regularly celebrated," but that rule, rigidly applied, would shut out such groups as Quakers and the Salvation Army, and Jesus would never do that. Some would say, "Any church that gives large sums to overseas missions," but that would sadly exclude those devout souls who have decided to give their alms at present to refugees rather than to missionaries. Some would say, "Any church where worship is sincerely offered," but the worship of some people never expresses itself in any kind of service to others, and something must be deficient there. Some will suggest, "A church rich in prayer meetings," but we all know that prayer meetings vary widely, and prayer is not so holy an occupation that it cannot be abused. This question is harder to answer than we thought: "What is a successful church?"

If the question were pressed on me, I think I would say, "Any church filled with the love that is the life of God." We know that "God is love" (1 John 4:8). "Filled" is the difficult word. A church is a public place; anyone can come. A malicious gossip might regularly attend a church and pump the poison of scandal into the fellowship of God's people, and there would be no easy way to prevent it. But if the central fellowship were "filled with the love that is the life of God," the poison would be sterilized. The "antibodies" in love would master the evil in the gossip, and the health of the body would be maintained. So let us stick to that definition for now: "A successful church is any church filled with the love that is the life of God."

It will be seen at once that this definition is related to the others. Love attracts; such a church is likely to grow. The holy table will be spread; Jesus Himself said, "Do this in remembrance of me." Overseas missions will be supported; Jesus said, "Go ye into all the world." Worship will be sincere, yet relate itself to service; God has bound together our love for Him and for our neighbors. Prayer meetings of the right kind will be common; Jesus said, "Where two or three are gathered together in my name. . . ." Yet no single consequence will do for a definition; a successful church is any church filled with the love that is the life of God.

How Can We Have Divine Love?

How many churches live up to this definition? Only God knows for sure. But in the secrecy of our hearts—remembering that when we judge our church we judge ourselves—we could at least ask some pertinent questions: Is my church filled with divine love? Are we a family in God, without class, monetary, or social distinctions? Does our love overflow to the community? Do the people who don't come know us as people who are always eager to help? Do our members stand out for integrity and kindness in all their walks of life? Does our existence as a church make an important difference for the best things in all the neighborhood? Are we interpreting God's love in some way to the wider world?

These are questions that seem to thrust at the heart of things. Take them slowly again. Answer them honestly, and be on your guard against any criticism but self-criticism. If your church is failing, put this question to yourself: What can I do about it?

It would be wrong for me to guess what God will say to you, but I am bound to admit that to me (and to most of my friends who have submitted to this test) He said at once, "How much of this love do you yourself have?" Then He began a most unhurried and loving probe. "Are you prone to criticism? to jealousy? to whining? Do most things that come up have an immediate self-reference in your mind? Are you unaware that resentment is no less poisonous for being justified? Is love going out of you all the time to other people? If it is my love you want flowing through you, you must learn that it is divinely possible to ache with love and pity over the most vicious and repulsive people, even while you hate their sin."

This kind of scrutiny from heaven, if a man will submit to it, can turn him inside out and make him a different kind of Christian from what he had ever dreamed. It isn't done in one session. It may take weeks of God's piercing light before you feel that every dark cavity has been explored. But the moment will come when you face in stark helplessness another question: How can I get this love? You will know you haven't got it. You will know how much you want it, for your church and for yourself. But how? Let me tell you that, and you will have the secret for yourself and for the church.

"Love that is the life of God" is a gift of God. You cannot get it by your own will, however strong. No sinner can say with sense, "Go to! I will have love." You cannot get it by reason. John Wesley said, "Reason cannot produce the love of God, so neither can it produce the love of our neighbor.

Love never flowed from any fountain but gratitude to our Creator."

If you want the way to love put into one word, it is the word *attend*. Attend to God in prayer. See Him as revealed by Jesus. Concentrate on that high part of prayer we call adoration. Just look . . . look . . . look. Longing will awake in you, and longing and loving in this context are almost indistinguishable.

Adoration is the major part of prayer among the holy. Personal petition has hardly any place; intercession has a large place; thanksgiving and confession are there; but adoration leads and shines and covers all the rest.

So we come to the deep principle which the mystics have long known and which guarantees the success of our quest: Looking, longing, loving, we grow like . . . (Repeat that phrase in all the intervals of this day until it is etched in your memory.) Divine love is a divine gift. It comes into us mainly in our private prayers and especially in that part of them we call adoration. As it fills us, we become like our Savior. A church made up of people growing like the Savior is a successful church, in the only way the word *successful* makes spiritual sense at all.

How can we transform a cold and lifeless church? Even when we have examined our hearts and privately resolved to seek God's glory, there remains our ingrained attitude toward divine service. Are we helping the service, or hindering it? How do we worship? How do we apply this love? Let us consider the church at prayer.

How Do We Pray at Church?

How do we pray at church? Do we enjoy the prayers, or find them boring? Are they full of inspiration and insight, or empty words beating the air? Does public prayer open the gates of heaven, or do we just endure the rush of words waiting as patiently as we can for the next hymn?

Prayer is the basis of all real worship. That is why even before the service begins, we bow in prayer as soon as we have taken our seats. Some people bow their heads because it is expected of them. (Is it really true that some count ten before sitting up again and looking around?) Some pray for the preacher, asking God to give him an inspiring message and the power to deliver it. Some pray for the worshipers, beseeching God to make them receptive and teachable. Some pray that God will enter the heart of a particular person for whom they care. Some pray for themselves out of their own deeply felt need.

A congregation that assembles before service time and uses these quiet moments in earnest prayer builds up a wonderful atmosphere that draws the very best out of a preacher. He feels it as he mounts the platform. It warms his heart and adds depth and significance to what he wants to say. Where such preliminary, private prayer is absent, there is a cold hardness that inhibits even the greatest preacher and makes it almost impossible for him to convey the truth and beauty he has seen. His message withers and dies in that prayerless air.

We sometimes condemn a man as a poor preacher when the fact is, we were a poor congregation; we never gave him a chance to show what he could do. Our unbelief and lack of spiritual vision cramped and trapped him into stilted phrases and dull platitudes. In an atmosphere of prayer, even the least gifted preacher is lifted up and inspired and becomes a vehicle for the word of God.

But what of public prayer? In all services there are several times of prayer. It is common to open with a hymn followed by a prayer. It is sometimes said that a good, substantial hymn gives the latecomers time to get in without disturbance so that the doors can be closed for the prayer.

That is not, of course, the purpose of the hymn. It is the opening act of praise, the glad pouring out of the heart's adoration. In some churches the hymn itself is preceded by an introit, in which the choir alerts us to the presence of God, or by a call to worship from the preacher. This emphasizes the function of the hymn as an act of worship. It is the united acclamation of God's greatness by His children. The hymn weds great language to great music. It is the best that we can produce; and the more we sing it, the more we see in it. The hymn carries us into the heavenly places and gives us glimpses of things unseen.

To many people, the prayer that follows that opening hymn is an anticlimax, four or five minutes of sheer boredom in which the mind wanders into its own dreams. Young people especially sometimes find it hard to endure and begin to whisper to one another or to reach for a stick of gum. Why? What is wrong with prayer? Nothing. It is the way it is done that is often wrong.

Why should a sermon addressed to ordinary men and women be interesting and full of thrilling thoughts, and a prayer addressed to God be so deadly dull? One reason may be that some preachers prepare their sermons with care, but think they can pray without a moment's preparation. This is due to a mistaken conception of prayer. It is assumed that God doesn't worry about grammar or even about coherence. All we have to do is just talk to Him naturally, to carry on an informal, casual, and entirely one-sided conversation, saying whatever comes into our heads.

God is probably as bored with such prayer as the people in the pew. He loves to hear the simple, unlettered prayers of children or the sincere outpourings of those unschooled in language who stammer out their adoration. But that does not mean that public worship must be conducted at the mental level of the preschooler or the semi-literate.

Many Christians prefer extemporaneous prayer to the read prayer, which they may dismiss as formal and lifeless. It is alleged that read prayers are often "recited." But a well-read prayer is at least one somebody has thought about and taken the trouble to compose. I believe all public prayer must be prepared in the sense that whoever undertakes to lead the people of God to the throne of grace ought to know what he intends to say and how he is going to say it. He speaks as the representative of the people. He has to sum up and express their devotion, love, hopes, needs. God is not impressed by flowery speech, so there is no need for "purple patches." But before he enters the church building, the preacher should have thought out what has to be said and how to say it in the clearest, fewest words.

The preacher's business is to pray for people who do not always know how to pray for themselves, so that as they listen to him they can say in their hearts, "Yes, Father, that is what I feel. He is speaking for me, Lord." A man who leads in prayer like that can lift the whole congregation to the threshold of heaven. And a congregation that prays like that cannot be static, apathetic, and introverted. It becomes vital, with a glowing fellowship and a burning desire to seek the lost.

One cannot be in any serious Methodist gathering for long without hearing the word *evangelism.* We are constantly told that this is the first business of the church and the reason why God raised us up. This is an oversimplification, but it emphasizes the important truth that a church that does not evangelize is dying and has lost its way. And a church does not evangelize unless the people pray.

The driving power of evangelism is a personal experience so vital and glowing that it is impossible to keep it to oneself. The realization of what Christ has done, the wonder of such amazing and costly love, the thrill of release from previous bondage and blindness—all these generate an irrepressible longing to tell the world.

In the narrow sense, an evangelist is a servant of Christ with a special gift. But in the widest sense we are all evangelists. We should all feel the evangelist's longing to bring friends and neighbors, workmates and casual acquaintances to our Lord. Day by day we should be quietly and persistently commending to them our Savior. We may not be able to speak in public meetings, but by unfailing friendliness, patience, understanding, and forgiving love we should be pointing people to Jesus.

This does not happen haphazardly. It needs careful planning in the secret place of prayer. It means thinking of people as individuals and praying for them in earnest intercession until God opens the way for us to speak the word that will bring them home.

If every prayer cell member would engage in intensive prayer, pleading before the mercy seat for one friend day after day, week in and week out, beseeching that God will bring him or her right into the fellowship of the church, I believe we would see the beginning of a new and glorious period of advance for the church of Christ.

Chapter 9

Prayer and Sickness

O Master, may I seek not so much to be comforted, as to comfort; not so much to be loved, as to love.
—St. Francis of Assisi

No one can read the Gospels thoughtfully and not be struck by the amount of space given to the healing miracles of our Lord. Christ appears always to have looked on sickness as a contradiction of His Father's perfect will, and to have met faith with a cure.

The power to convey the direct healing of God was passed on to the apostles also, but appears to have been half-lost in the early centuries of church history. Even anointing for healing became largely anointing for death, and the rite of extreme unction is administered now only when doctors have almost abandoned hope. Spectacular healings have occurred in connection with the Christian faith all through the centuries, but they have been rare and wonderful. It is only in recent years that the subject has been opened up afresh and books (of varying value) have been poured out on the theme.

It is not our purpose here to go deeply into this subject, but the ministry of prayer cells requires some mention of it. We must pray for those who are physically sick: (1) because of our sympathy and compassion and their great need, (2) because faith is nourished by prayer, and faith assists healing as certainly as fear hinders it, (3) because medical science now recognizes that many diseases begin in the mind and spirit (though they seriously affect the body), and their healing can begin in the mind and spirit too, and (4) because there are instances of organic disease being suddenly cured in ways which no doctors can yet explain, but which (in the opinion of the devout and of some doctors) appear to be direct acts of God. I have stated these reasons carefully and, I hope, uncontroversially. The only one still subject to debate is point 4.

Mental Illness

Sickness is always sad, but there is none so sad as mental illness. It seems to take our dear ones from us in a way that physical sickness never does. When their minds are deranged or confused, a curtain hangs between us, and fellowship is hindered or destroyed.

Some people are half-ashamed when their relatives become mentally ill. They mention it either not at all or only as a guilty secret. They often have to fight awful fears within themselves of "tainted blood" or "bad heredity." This is why so many people in mental hospitals have "no known relatives." Most of them have relatives of course, but they are not known. They don't want to be known. They seem to think that there is a disgrace in the sickness and that the disgrace attaches in part to them.

All this only adds to the sadness of it. To be ill is hard, but to be ill and shunned is terrible. It makes recovery all the harder, too. No intelligent person denies today that there is healing power in love. A mentally ill person may not be conscious of love, but it blesses them (when they have it) at a deeper level than the conscious mind. The thought that thousands of people are lying in hospitals and are robbed of that ministration from their relatives moves one to compassion and prayer for the chance to help.

Mental sickness is no more disgraceful than any other sickness. Indeed, it is usually far less disgraceful than venereal disease or the D.T.'s. It affects some of the loveliest, most intelligent, and sophisticated people in the community. I have visited in mental hospitals for nearly forty years and I speak of what I know.

Moreover, the idea of some people that this sickness is never completely cured is nonsense. There are people doing magnificent work in all walks of life and in ebullient health who have been mentally ill and have spent long terms in mental hospitals. One can find them in government, medical careers, the ordained ministry, law, teaching, and skilled trades.

Nor can we underestimate the size of this need. Half the hospital beds in the Western world are occupied by people with mental or nervous disorders. It is all the more sad that, in comparison with some other forms of disease, so little is spent on the research that might (under God) bring healing to millions.

Never forget to pray for medical research workers in all branches of healing. They are God's agents whether they know it or not. I used to sit next to Sir Alexander Fleming on the Senate of the University of London, and I know the gratitude he felt in discovering penicillin and bringing help to multitudes. We want major discoveries in mental sickness, too, and in pleading for prayer for these sufferers, I slip in this plea for those who are doing high research in the diseases of the mind.

But let us deal with the matter at hand. We have a vocation to pray. How does prayer relate to mental sickness? In very special ways.

We know that faith in the mind of a person suffering from physical sickness is a channel of healing. But people with a confused or diseased mind are often incapable of such faith. Are they cut off from divine healing because of this?

Some of the most loving letters I have received come from a woman in a mental hospital who has periods of complete lucidity. In such times she is sure that God could heal her, but for years the periods of darkness have descended. Her written pleas for prayer support would move the heart of the most selfish person. And behind her I see a vast company in similar need.

Our Lord seems always to have sought faith in the mind of those who came to Him seeking healing, but He sometimes healed without it, or at least He took the faith of friends for the faith of the sick. You remember the paralyzed man carried to Christ by four determined friends: "When Jesus saw *their* faith . . ." (Mark 2:5).

I plead for that kind of faith and prayer for the mentally ill whom you know. Because of the character of their sickness, their need is greater and their capacity for faith less. Believe for them. See them well. Picture them fit, happy, busy for God; and pray your desire. God cannot be glorified by mental disease. It is ugly, horrible, and some of it quite satanic. Send out every day a stream of love and faith toward the mentally ill. Though the months and years go by without the full answer to your prayers, don't give up. If you grow weary thinking of them, how must it be with them who are bearing it! Never give up.

Ralph had been in the mental hospital for years. He was considered "hopeless"—an awful thing to say of anyone. But our long prayers saw improvement, and the glad time came when Ralph was allowed to come out for weekends. One grand Christian couple always had him in their home and brought him to our church. Then he was declared healed and discharged. He wrote to say that one thing that helped him in the long months as he was recovering was a line he heard me quote from a hymn of Charles Wesley:

"Jesus, Thou art all compassion." The day came when the compassionate Jesus broke through and made him whole.

How to Pray for the Sick

But how should we pray for the sick? It is not a silly question. It comes from people who are growing in prayer (and want to grow more) and feel that reeling names off to God, as one runs down a list in the telephone directory, is not a mature or effective way to pray. What can we say that will help them pray better for the sick?

Concern for the sick does not mean pestering the relatives for news, but rather wrapping the sufferers, and those who most love them, tight in a God-given love. Select people you know, or who are known to some other member of the prayer cell. Get all the facts you can. We have often found it helpful to have or see a photograph of the person we are praying for. Concentrate your concern on one or two particular people.

Praying for the sick—especially for those with a disease for which medical science still has found no cure—is very testing to patience. But it is a good deal more testing to the sick, so don't fail in patience. Theirs is the heavier load.

Prayer hasn't completely failed if the sick do not swiftly recover. If it helps them in the meantime to bear the load with courage, hope, and trust, and without complaint, self-pity, or despair, prayer hasn't failed, and greater things may yet come.

Don't try to reproduce in yourself the feelings that you imagine your sick friends endure. You won't succeed, and you may do yourself harm.

Before interceding for the sick, spend time thinking about God and His love, mercy, and power; then just draw your sick friends in their need into His presence. Hold God and your friends together in your warm, believing heart.

If you had a friend who was ill, you would gladly give an

hour to visiting him. But he might live too far away to do that. Even if he lived near, he might be too ill to have visitors or too tired to maintain prolonged talk. Why not give the whole hour to prayer?

Does the idea strike you as absurd? A whole hour—to one friend? But you would have given him more than an hour, counting traveling time, to visit him. It can't be the time you begrudge. Is it more important to talk to him than to talk to God about him? What wonderful things do you have to say to your sick friend that can compare with what God might say to him? Sometimes a visit is just right. But what modest mortal can really believe that his help can compare with the help of the holy God?

Forbes Robinson once said that in his younger days he had taken every opportunity to appeal personally to men to come to Christ. Then he added, "As I grow older I become more diffident, and now often, when I desire the Truth to come home to any man, I say to myself: 'If I have him here, he will spend half an hour with me. Instead I will spend half an hour in prayer for him.'" This was part of the secret of Robinson's astonishing spiritual power. He was thinking of evangelism; you are thinking of your sick friend. The same principle could apply. Don't dream for a moment that this is a criticism of all sick visitation; God is using that lovely ministry every day. But it isn't always possible and it isn't always best. Prayer is always possible, and nothing can surpass it in worth.

Let us suppose that you have reserved an hour or a half-hour for prayer. What will you do then?

Get alone. Go to your room and shut the door. "Pray to the Father in secret," Jesus said. Compose yourself in God's presence. Be quiet and unhurried within. Feel like a person with "all the time in the world."

Think on God. The way to think on God, of course, is to think on Him as revealed by Jesus: loving people whether they have been good or not, forgiving and full of compassion, always meeting penitence with pardon. See Him always responsive to the cry and moving out in healing to the sick.

Then think on your sick friend. Be careful not to dwell so vividly on the symptoms of his sickness that imaginatively you reproduce them in yourself. Visualize him as well, happy, buoyant. Compassion will grow in your heart.

This compassion is most important. It gives lift and power to prayer in a way that duty can't. Let your mind move from God to your friend, and from your friend to God, while this compassion gets deeper and deeper. It doesn't matter if twenty-five of your thirty minutes goes this way—or fifty-five of the sixty. The moment will come when you seem able to hold together in the crucible of your longing heart the readiness of God to bless and the readiness of your friend to receive. All your plea can go into the minutes that remain.

You may learn later of the effect of your prayer, or you may not. No matter. Don't fidget for daily confirmation. Such praying can't fail to bless. You may not see a swift, dramatic healing, but the blessing has gone into your friend's spirit and through that will reach his body in some way. Unknown to you, while you are praying, he may be fighting waves of depression and finding faith especially hard. And—suddenly—there are reinforcements coming to his aid; faith revives and fear is beaten, and you have been the channel by which the blessing has come.

Nobody knows of this ministry but God and you. There is no human notice of it and no public praise. Better so. You will not suspect your own motives in doing it; it is being done for love, and for love alone.

It is almost by accident that I have learned of people in our prayer cells with this great vocation of prayer. I did not learn of it from them. Some of them don't know I know. It is the effect of their prayers that can't be hid.

Never toss the responsibility of believing for healing back on the sick person himself. Some "healers" do; they almost nag the sick: "If you only had enough faith, you'd be healed." But without minimizing the importance of faith in the sick person, the compassionate people of prayer gladly take the role of the four men who let their paralyzed friend down at the feet of Jesus and believe for him. They stand on God's promises and don't "spiritualize" them away until they mean nothing. "If ye abide in me, and my words abide in you, ye shall ask what ye will . . ." (John 15:7). They abide in Him, and they ask. They don't lecture the fainting soul about "abiding." They may proffer tender guidance on how to think and how to pray, but the heavier part they take themselves. They *abide*. They rise early to pray and even have an arrangement with God to call them at any hour of the night for intercession. The answers many of them receive are quite wonderful.

I have sometimes wondered how they remain so serene with such costly service, but I know the answer to that now. When divine love flows through a human heart, it blesses not only the one to whom it flows but the channel it courses through.

Perhaps when you asked for help in praying for the sick, you hardly expected the standard to be set as high as this. Don't let me discourage you.

There are those who have a special vocation to pray, but it is good for us all to remember that in whatever class of the school of prayer we may be, there are classes beyond. People compassed about with much service may not be able to give hours to praying, but many retired people make this the major part of their service to God, and they are almost certainly the most effective people in the community.

Chapter 10

Spiritual Exercises

Hypocrites never pray in secret.
—Samuel Chadwick

Exercise is necessary for a healthy body. Exercise is essential for a growing mind. Remember your school books? Each fresh lesson ends with an exercise. By working at the exercises you master the subject.

Exercise is necessary for the growing soul. The life of prayer is mastered only by diligent application. Spiritual exercise takes the flabbiness out of the soul and superficiality out of prayer.

On a seaside vacation I watched a man who drove up every morning before anyone else was about, went down to the empty beach, quickly undressed, and then plunged into the sea. In a little while he returned, dressed as methodically as he had stripped, got into his car, and drove away. This was his morning exercise, and how he loved it! Rain or shine, there he was.

The man of prayer prays likes that: methodically. He gets ready for prayer by a swift, effective routine. Some people begin with the phrase "Let us recollect the presence of God." This is an admonition to remember that God actually exists, even though we may have forgotten Him.

Preparing to Meet God

When I was a young minister working in the slums of London, an older minister advised me, "You will go into many filthy hovels and dreadful places. Remember, God was there before you came and He will be there after you have gone." He was warning me to "recollect the presence," not only in the holy place, but in the unholy place. He wanted me to be constantly aware of that deeper dimension in which God is recognized.

But the injunction to "recollect the presence" can be very inadequate if all it means is a reminder that in our busy life we may have overlooked God. If that is an invitation to prayer, it is beginning at the wrong end. Instead we should begin by warning ourselves of what is about to happen if we intend to seek God. We should prepare to meet our God.

Occasionally we might still see—if only in cartoons—a man carrying sandwich boards bearing the text "Prepare to meet thy God." Some people dismiss him as a crank or fanatic; others feel a bit embarrassed by what they think is mild religious mania; some take the phrase to be a warning of impending doom and frankly disbelieve it. The words come from the message of Amos, and the prophet is asking Israel to realize what God is really like and to prepare itself for meeting Him.

> Prepare to meet thy God, O Israel.
> For, lo, he that formeth the mountains, and createth the wind, and declareth unto man what is his thought, that maketh the morning darkness, and treadeth upon the high places of the earth, The Lord. The God of hosts, is his name (Amos 4:12–13).

God is not inconsequential or remote. He is working in time and space. He is Lord of history, molding the world in which we live and pressing in on us from every side. But the most astonishing fact about God is that He *is*. It is His being—what He is in Himself—that is the permanent fascination of the life of prayer.

God's existence does not depend on our recollection. Our existence does depend upon His. Thus, when we turn to prayer, it is not so much a question of recollecting God but of preparing to meet Him, adjusting our minds and hearts to His greatness. The true recollection begins as we humbly draw near to this wonderful and glorious God, reminding ourselves, as Augustine said, that "God is wholly in every place, included in no place, not bound with cords (save those of love), not divided into parts, not changeable into several shapes, filling heaven and earth with His present power, and with His never absent nature" (*The City of God*, 7.30).

Jeremy Taylor, in a passage on the presence of God in *Holy Living and Dying*, puts the same majestic truth in a different way: "So we may imagine God to be as the air and the sea and we all enclosed in His circle, wrapt up in the lap of His infinite Nature, or as infants in the warmth of their pregnant mothers, and we can no more be removed from the presence of God than from our own being."

John Mason sings of this majesty that angel hosts adore:

> Thou art a sea without a shore,
> A sun without a sphere;
> Thy time is now and evermore,
> Thy place is everywhere.

When this is the posture of our spirits, then true worship begins.

Spiritual Exercises

The first preparation for prayer, therefore, is like the stripping down of the swimmer. Here is a simple exercise that will quickly make you ready for prayer:

- —Be quiet. Deliberately check the flow of impetuous and inconsequential thoughts.
- —Remember that you live in a big world among thousands of millions of people. But the world itself is little, a tiny speck in the galaxy.
- —Remember that God is greater than the universe. He is lord of the infinitely big and of the infinitely small.
- —Think of God's wisdom, power, and love at work every moment, sustaining all things everywhere.
- —Think of God holding you in His hands. Feel that love surrounding you. This is the majesty you seek.

Such directed thought is not easy at first, but soon you will acquire the ability to meditate, that is, to contemplate a truth and let its meaning possess you. You will need more exercises to bring other spiritual muscles under control. The man of prayer is a man who has mastered all the elements of his training.

A few minutes of private self-examination is another excellent preliminary exercise. Submit yourself to the check-up that follows. Do this unhurriedly for yourself and offer it to any Christian friends who feel no impulse to join a prayer cell. Take the questions slowly and only move on to the next when you have made honest reply.

- —Christ felt the need to spend many hours in prayer. Why don't I feel that way?
- —There are 960 wakeful minutes in my normal day. How many do I spend in pure prayer?
- —Christ has given His pledged word to be among two or three gathered in His name. Don't I want to be in His company?
- —There is no known instance of high quality of Christian character without much prayer. Don't I want that quality of character?
- —There is no known instance of a revival of religion without a wide prelude of prayer. Don't I want a revival of religion?

If you practice this exercise for a few weeks, each time going deeper and deeper into the questions, your whole spiritual condition will be tuned up. You will begin to face the realities of prayer and to learn the art of meditation. You are exposing yourself to the light of God.

You will then want to know more about God for Himself. Here is an exercise to help you to receive divine love. Get alone. Anywhere will do, but a quiet room where you are least likely to be disturbed is best. There are always things waiting to be done, of course, but choose a time when there is nothing that can't wait; the busiest people can find such times. Don't live as though everyone is more important to you than God. Kneel—if you can kneel for half an hour and still forget the body. Sit—if you can sit and not "lounge." Lie down—if you can lie and remain "passively alert."

You are alone.

Turn your thoughts fully on God.

He is always with you, but you so often forget.

He cannot give Himself to you until you give your mind to Him.

Give your whole mind to Him now.

Think on Him as revealed by Jesus:

  Holy—but eager to forgive penitent sinners (John 6:37)
  Wise—and ready to give His wisdom to you (James 1:5)
  Perfect—and longing that you share His perfection (Matt. 5:48)
  Loving—and wanting to pour His love through your heart (John 17:26)

Lift your whole personality to His. Steadily "stay" your entire mind on God.

Just gaze. There's no need to talk.

Ask for nothing.

Say nothing.

Want nothing.

Just look . . . and look . . . on your loving God.

Let the words of prayer come now if they will. Your own words are best, but let them lead you to adoration.

Father, revealed in Jesus, resident in the Spirit, do You love me like that—creating me, dying for me, living in me, loving me more than my dearest? I adore You. This, then, is the secret of the universe. Love burns at its heart. Let it burn in my heart, purging my sin, uniting me with You, reaching to all. Father! Jesus! Holy Spirit!

Only love to me be given.
Lord, I ask no other heaven. Amen.

Don't hurry away. Wait for the "signal." Feel this love burning in you. Only go when He bids you. And now, with that burning heart, return to your next duty.

A Pattern for Morning Prayer

The members of prayer groups are at many different stages of spiritual development. Some are really beginners; they have never prayed in their lives, or not since childhood. They say to themselves, "You must begin with the ABC's." Many find ten minutes too long and wonder what to talk about. Thus the simple outlines of prayer that follow may be useful. Don't be rigid with them. They are only suggestions; change them however you like.

If at first you don't feel like praying, prepare your mind by reading a passage of Scripture or a favorite hymn. Then as you warm up you can use this pattern for morning prayer.

Adoration

Everything ultimately depends on God. Adore Him. He is like Jesus. He is infinitely loving, infinitely wise. Every breath we draw, we draw by His permission. He even lends the atheist breath to deny Him. Think how awful it would be if there were no God, or if a devil were lord. Think of God as revealed by Jesus, and just adore Him in your heart.

Thanksgiving

How much you have to be thankful for! Review your blessings in your mind. Health? (Some health at least.) Love? Home? No great money worries (you make ends meet, don't you?). Children? Grandchildren? Good books? Flowers? Friends? Heap them together. Most days bring something extra, too. Note it for thanksgiving.

Dedication

Solemnly give yourself afresh to God every day.

> High heaven, that heard that solemn vow,
> That vow renewed shall daily hear.

Guidance

Think through your whole day, as far as you can foresee it, slowly with God. "This, that . . . this, that . . ." Meet each foreseeable experience with God before you meet it in reality. As time passes, you may get little warnings or "alerts." Increase your sensitivity to God's will for you, by exposing yourself more and more to His presence.

Intercession

Pray for others. Don't leave them to the casual recollection of the moment. Have lists. What better use for the back pages of your diary? Don't reel the names off like a list in the telephone directory. Unhurriedly intercede.

Petition

Is there something you want for yourself? Here is the place for it: last and least.

A Pattern for Evening Prayer

Here is a pattern for evening devotions.

Guard against coming to evening prayers too tired. It affronts the majesty of heaven to fall asleep over prayer.

Prepare for the closing devotions of the day by getting a quiet mind and thinking of God. A Bible reading often brings you right into His conscious presence.

Now, beginning just where you are, go back in thought over your day. (There's a sound psychological reason why it's best to go backward, but we needn't go into that.) Picture Christ at your side, and undertake the review with Him. There will be much to be thankful for: strength for work, warning of dangers, fellowship with friends, your senses, flowers, fun, home, dear ones. There may be some things to be sad about: warnings ignored, impatience, harsh and wounding words, coldness to someone who had a right to expect warmth, showing off, neglected duties. It is surprising how honest, thorough, and quick this review can become when it is built into daily practice. It provides the substance of your evening prayer.

Confession

Examine your sins in confession. Use no clichés: "Forgive me all my sins." Say *what* sins. Name the dirty things and blush over them. Remember the missed opportunities of doing good; tell them to God. (If He tells you to apologize or make some restitution, note it and get it done as soon as you can.) Wait for His word of forgiveness. *Wait.* If it doesn't come at the snap of a finger, still wait. (You'll get a little more ashamed as you wait.) When you know yourself forgiven for this daily defilement, move on to thanksgiving.

Thanksgiving

Now loosen your tongue. What a loving Father you have! Remember all the things noted in the review for gratitude. Thank Him. Pour it out—for this and that, this and that. You were unaware of the special, divine origin of many blessings, so you had best include gratitude for them also.

Intercession

The serious intercession of the day has been offered earlier, but on most days there are urgent needs you feel you must mention again; mention them now.

Before sleeping

Our last thoughts often affect our dreams and sometimes are our first on waking. Therefore choose them. The brain goes on "working" even while we sleep. Feed the right thoughts to it such as a couplet from a hymn:

> Safe in Thy arms I lay me down,
> Thy everlasting arms of love.

Or picture a scene from the gospels: Jesus healing or blessing or teaching. Or picture yourself, utterly relaxed, utterly clean by His forgiveness, being divinely restored as you sleep. Or picture a good day tomorrow.

A Meditation on the Incarnation

A meditation on the holy mystery of the Incarnation is a much more strenuous exercise. It needs plenty of time; to hurry it is to destroy its usefulness. Each line needs consideration. The asterisks that follow each section indicate a step forward in the sequence of thought. There should be a pause while the thoughts of the preceding section are summed up and driven home.

But first, a few instructions for those who are unfamiliar with this method. The exercise is not meant to be read through quickly; each direction should be followed by a period of meditation in which you firmly compel your mind to contemplate the suggested thought.

Like physical exercise, this meditation should be repeated regularly and frequently. To do it once and leave it will probably only give you spiritual stiffness; to do it regularly will make the spirit strong and flexible. If you continue the exercise two or three times a week for three months, you will find that the thoughts become a quiet background to your daily living, like distant music which, far from distracting, inspires you to greater efficiency. Be quiet. Relax. Wait on God. Steadily will your way into the stillness.

Silent am I now and still,
Dare not in Thy presence move;
To my waiting soul reveal
The secret of Thy love.

*　　*　　*

Think of the ineffable Being of God, the almighty, the perfect, the glorious One.

*　　*　　*

Think of God as the joyful Creator,
Fashioning all the galaxies.
Picture these star cities of outer space,
Declaring the glory of God.

*　　*　　*

Fasten your gaze now on this solar system;
Pick out this tiny planet we call Earth
Spinning in its orbit around the golden sun.
Think of it as it left the hands of God,
This globe which He prepared to be the home of man.

*　　*　　*

What went wrong?
What dark malignant power usurped this holy sphere?
Why did the prince of the world rebel against his Lord?
What was it that deflected man from the way of holiness?
Why did man allow himself to be deceived?
Why is each still the Adam of his own soul?

*   *   *

Think now of the rejected Lord of man:
Feel the sorrow of God,
Spurned and forgotten by self-sufficient man.
Consider God's repudiated love.
Was ever sorrow like His sorrow?

*   *   *

What will God do to the disobedient planet?
Will He blot it out of His holy universe?
How long will He tolerate the spawning sin of earth—
The lies, the greed, the lust, the pride of men?

*   *   *

Penetrate into the hidden counsel of God.
What does His holy righteousness say to the sin of man?
Behold Him sending messenger after messenger;
Mark their reception by rebellious man.

*   *   *

Who is this that comes forth from the heart of the Eternal?
It is the Beloved,
The Son, true God of true God,
Who invades the sin-bound earth,
Not to destroy, but to save.
His beachhead is Bethlehem.
He takes our flesh. His name is Jesus.

*   *   *

What manner of love is this?
Earth, the dark and silent planet,
Is now the visited planet.
The Light shone here.
The heaven of heavens has seen nothing like this.

*　　*　　*

Will the great plan succeed?
Will earth receive its Lord?
Will it become the paradise it should have been?

*　　*　　*

See what we did to the Holy One.
Our darkness could not, would not, comprehend.
See Him mocked, derided.
See Him stretched on yonder Cross.
Gaze, soul, on the crucified God.
Break, break, O stubborn heart.

*　　*　　*

Now see Him, the Risen Lord,
His glorious work accomplished,
Back in the eternal glory.
Feel now the power He freely gives
To every contrite, believing heart.

*　　*　　*

Know thyself twice-bought, O my soul,
By thy Maker and Redeemer.
Thou art His forever, only His,
No longer thine own.

*　　*　　*

Live then through Him.
For love's sake, live this day with Him.
For Christ's sake, live this day for Him.
Blessed be God.
Amen and amen.

When a prayer cell uses these exercises, the leader should read out each line slowly, leaving time for meditation before he reads the next. At the major pauses he can sum up the thought of the passage in a brief sentence or two of prayer.

Similar exercises can be compiled around the great themes of the faith. Many of the great Wesley hymns are also splendid spiritual exercises and can be used in this way.

Taking Time to Pray

These meditations thrill the soul as they open up to us the glories of God's grace. We will find we want to give more time to prayer. Where can we find that time?

In addition to the public prayers of the church, members of prayer cells approach prayer in three ways: (1) they have a firm scheme of daily private prayer, (2) they share in the life of the cell, and (3) they learn to use for communion with God all kinds of unexpected moments—for example, waiting for a bus, brief travel time, waiting to be served in a crowded restaurant. They don't make a burden of it. Prayer becomes their joy and inner life.

These "vacant" moments in the day can be dangerous. When the mind isn't concentrated, it often opens itself to fears—fears of sickness, failure, loss of love. All kinds of debilitating things can creep in. If we were thinking only of ourselves, we would learn how to guard against these times of fantasy-thought lest they lead to personal harm.

But avoiding harm is not the main purpose in the minds of people who are deeply interested in prayer. That is only a welcome by-product. Loving God as they do, they want to be consciously with Him whenever they can. These unexpected moments are not times to fume because the bus or waiter won't come, but times to use in healthy, happy communion with the One who becomes dearer with every passing year.

Let us use these moments. Let us have in the vestibule of our minds noble words to meditate upon: love, joy, peace, patience (Gal. 5:22–23). Someday we may even enjoy being kept waiting!

A half-hour of quiet sitting in a garden can be wonderful. No, don't read. Look—and think of God. Brother Lawrence was converted looking at a tree. Just look! There are some ugly things in nature, of course, but look now at the flowers. Think of the cycle of the seasons. Think of growth.

Music is a medium of God to many people and would be to many more if they would take the trouble to listen. The music needs to be selected according to taste and understanding. But a half-hour of listening to the right music and thinking on God can open heaven to a reverent mind.

Do you like maps? They fascinate me. I often have a session of prayer with maps. When I prayed for college students on evangelistic campaigns, I usually had a map in front of me. I had a list of the places and the people. I put my finger on the spot on the map, pictured the situation from the information I possessed, thought on the men and women, and prayed a blessing on all their enterprise.

Do you ever pray with the stars? Some night when you are not too tired, turn out the light before getting into bed and look at the stars. What awe there is in the night sky! No wonder Immanuel Kant found his way back to God by "the moral law within and the starry heavens without." Just look—and commune with the God who made them all.

These are just some of the ways to find time to pray. Find your own, but be sure you find them. You want to be like your Lord, and all His life was prayer and love.

Chapter 11

The Higher Reaches of Prayer

Prayer is the essence of the test of the godly life.
—Samuel Chadwick

In this chapter we try to deal more fully with the higher reaches of prayer. These aspects of the devotional life are apt to be viewed with suspicion by some Christians. They fear that the practice of intensive and especially interior prayer may lead to unhealthy introspection, exaggerated other-worldliness, or priggish piety.

These are real dangers, and such undesirable results are inevitable when our motives are wrong. If our aim is to seek strange experiences and ecstatic feelings, or to make ourselves objects of admiration, then we can expect disastrous effects on character.

But we must not allow the misuse of prayer to deter us from the wonderful joys God has in store for those who pursue the path of prayer. The aim of true Christian prayer is fellowship with God. When the heart earnestly seeks God for Himself and not just for His gifts, when it longs to make itself acceptable to Him, then the arduous pursuit of the life of advanced prayer is altogether right and proper.

There was a time when the heirs of John Wesley's movement knew a great deal about these deeper experiences. Simple men and women trained and encouraged each other in the inner disciplines of the soul. They were mighty in prayer. I believe that such mighty prayer, which alone makes saints, is desperately needed in the church today. Nothing else can bring into this hard, material age the convincing evidence of the deeper dimensions that underlie human life and make God real.

This prayer is not escapist as some suggest. On the contrary, few people have had such impact on the world of their day as the great heroes of faith. They shattered the smug complacencies of their age, enlarged horizons, overthrew massive indifference, and brought sanity, sweetness, vision, and hope to their generation.

Beyond the Spoken Word

We begin to make progress when we realize that there are great ranges of experience beyond the limits of vocal prayer. It is surprising how many Christian people believe that prayer consists entirely of the spoken word. We habitually think of people "saying" their prayers, as if prayer was never more than uttered thanksgiving, adoration, petition, confession, and intercession.

Bede Frost rightly insists in *The Art of Mental Prayer* that it is quite possible to maintain vocal prayer for years without any growth in grace, without ever dreaming that there is a great new world waiting to be explored beyond the spoken word.

If ever we are to develop spiritually and get beyond a superficial religiosity, we must deliberately make up our minds that we are not going to be content until we know God for Himself. That experience is really indescribable. No words can express it, no picture is adequate, no symbol is sufficient. How could it be?

Speech has been devised for human occasions. It can be fairly accurate in naming objects and fairly precise in measuring things; but when we turn from things to persons, language is near its limits. Who does not grope vainly for the right words to convey his profoundest thoughts, his richest and strongest feelings? How often we are compelled to admit defeat and appeal helplessly for understanding, exclaiming, "You know what I mean!" We are counting on the likelihood that others have had similar experiences and will recognize what we mean. But how often they misunderstand and we turn away baffled and inarticulate!

The old Chinese peasant in Pearl Buck's classic novel, *The Good Earth,* says to his dying wife, whose worth he has just begun to realize, "If a man had words, there are things to be said." But we haven't the words. Our deepest feelings and most personal experiences defy expression. Poets and singers with their mastery of language may get a little nearer, but the most skillful artist knows that there are thoughts too deep for words. Tongue cannot utter nor pen express the range and quality of our greatest experiences.

If, then, language fails us at the very point where we most long to be understood, how can it possibly describe our experiences of God?

> But what to those who find? Ah! this
> Nor tongue nor pen can show:
> The love of Jesus, what it is
> None but His loved ones know.

Because prayer generates the atmosphere in which these experiences usually occur, we must expect to reach a point where words no longer suffice. At this moment prayer becomes silent. I mean here something quite different from what is usually meant by "silent prayer." When silent prayer is called for in a church service, it generally means thinking in words without uttering them; often you can see the lips moving. But the prayer of silence is not thought or expressed in words at all; it goes far beyond them.

Instead of asking for things, interceding for others, or just talking to God, we find ourselves contemplating a single idea, some great truth about His being that rivets our attention. The mind ranges over it, discovering new wonders and unsuspected depths. Some of the ideas that come to us we could express in words, but only later, not at the moment of contemplation. Much that we see we know we can never express in human speech; we should need a new language and a new type of mind to comprehend it.

This kind of interior prayer begins in fleeting moments. If we give it the deliberate attention it deserves, it will steadily increase in importance in our prayer life. The moments will grow longer. Not that we shall ever cease to pray in words— we shall still make our petitions, offer praise and thanksgiving, and intercede constantly; but more and more we will want to give time to this prayer of silence when we are content to gaze on some aspect of God's glorious being.

Beyond Mysticism

As we grow accustomed to interior prayer, there will eventually be times when even the mind ceases to be active. It will leave its probing, exploring, and wondering. There will be periods when we are suddenly aware of nothing but God Himself and the sweetness of His love. In utter silence we fall before Him, the creature in the presence of the Creator.

It is right and proper to cultivate this life of prayer. Those who remain content with the prayer of words are missing some of the profoundest joys God wants to give.

> But sweeter than the honey jar
> The glimpses of His presence are.

Both this quotation and the preceding one come from a devotional poem by Bernard of Clairvaux. Sometimes these experiences are dismissed as medieval mysticism and therefore hallucinatory. This is a sad mistake. Every religion has its mysticism; but Christian mysticism is quite different from that of other faiths, for it is centered in Christ. Protestant as well as Catholic saints have known this joy. It is God's gift to us all in Jesus.

Dr. Victor Murray opens his book *Personal Experience and the Historic Faith* with an extract from the diary of Agnes Beaumont, a young servant girl who in 1674 rode behind John Bunyan to a Baptist meeting at Gaminglay.

> After a while the meeting began and God made it a blessed meeting to my soul indeed. . . . My soul was filled with consolation and I sat under His Shadow with great delight. . . . I found such a return of prayer that I was scarce able to bear up under it. Oh, I had such a sight of Jesus Christ it breaks my heart to pieces! . . . A sense of my sins, and of His dying love made me love Him and long to be with Him.

Agnes Beaumont was only twenty-two, an unlearned English maid, but her experience and that of St. Bernard are the same. All who through the centuries have thus experienced Jesus would recognize that "sweetness and light" that combines with "the breaking of the heart" that Agnes tries to describe.

You are invited to these joys of interior prayer. The feast is there and many guests have been summoned, yet it is surprising how many find excuses to stay away. But for those who are prepared to seek the face of God, to walk the path of prayer, for them the feast is spread in the quiet chambers of the soul.

> The o'erwhelming power of saving grace,
> The sight that veils the seraph's face:
> The speechless awe that dares not move,
> And all the silent heaven of love.

Beyond Struggle

One of the greatest dangers of Protestantism is its tendency to reduce all spiritual effort to a struggle for moral perfection. We have so deeply felt the reality of sin that we have interpreted religion as the great remedy for evil and we measure our growth in grace by our ability to overcome temptations.

There is, of course, a profound truth in this, for the Christian is one who has broken away from the fetters of evil. A religious life that does not make a person better is not worth having. But this is not the whole truth, and unless it is carefully watched it can become a perilous heresy. As the apostle Paul realized, the Christian way is not primarily a moral struggle at all, but an acceptance. It is not what we achieve, but what God gives that saves us (Rom. 7:17–25; Eph. 2:8).

The struggle for righteousness—which we can never win—must give way to a thirst for God. Prayer must become not so much a plea for victory and strength as the simple act of "exposing our will to the warmth of heavenly love," as St. Francis de Sales describes it (*Introduction to the Devout Life*, 2.1).

Let us be clear on this. On the one hand, I am saying that no man is justified by works. We don't become saints by moral effort. On the other hand, faith without works is dead and useless (James 2:17–26). A living faith must express itself in moral effort. This is a paradox, but that really means it is a spiritual truth beyond language and linguistic logic. Nor is this just an old, dry-as-dust theological argument. The truth we are seeking can be approached another way.

We have said that the Christian way is primarily one of acceptance. It is the gift of God. But nothing is quite so hard to accept as a gift from God. For one thing, it means coming with an empty hand, and that is not easy for the proud human spirit. We always like to feel we have somehow deserved God's gift or at least done something to merit His grace. But to know we have done nothing except misunderstand, ignore, and misjudge Him, to know that our whole life must be hideous with blemishes in His holy sight, to know that we can never be fit by our own efforts to draw near to Him—that fills us with the painful humility of penitence and shame.

"Nothing in my hands I bring." That is the attitude of interior prayer. The labor is not just a moral effort, but a spiritual one in which we compel the real self, from which we have been running all our lives, to halt, turn about, and seek for God.

You cannot put this into words, for you are dealing with levels of being for which there are no words. But that does not mean they do not exist. Prayer knows that they do, and it explores these levels where is prayed the unutterable prayer of the Spirit (Romans 8:26). So make time in your prayers for the prayer of silence, a prayer that can never be said.

The essence of this type of prayer is the determination to seek God for Himself. It is not easy, especially in the early stages, because the mind is wayward, the will is weak, and the body dislikes the discipline of deliberate inactivity. But to those who persevere, the prize is great. For when God comes, He alters the balance and integration of the whole personality and brings a new and heavenly harmony into our discordant lives. A moment comes when our eager wills identify themselves gladly with His holy will, no matter what the cost. And in that sacred moment we know that "in a love which cannot cease, I am His and He is mine."

Samuel John Stone expresses in a hymn the acceptance of the gift of pardon and the attitude of utter humility:

> O great Absolver, grant my soul may wear
> The lowliest garb of penitence and prayer,

That in the Father's courts my glorious dress
May be the garment of Thy righteousness.

Beyond Longing

Some years ago I stood in the old marketplace of South Shields with a dear old man who pointed down a narrow back street and said:

When I was about nineteen I stood here one Saturday night. The market was in full swing, with the crowds milling round the stalls in the light of the naphtha flares. But in spite of the noise and bustle I felt alone, and a great hunger for prayer possessed me. I recalled that there was a little chapel down that back street, and I wondered if it might still be open even at that late hour. So I went down the dark lane and saw a chink of light and a half-open door. It led me upstairs to a small room at the back of the chapel. The room was half full and a prayer meeting was going on. I sat among them and noticed how poor they were, men and women in old thread-bare clothes with the lines of poverty in their faces. But as they prayed for the services next day, and laid their hearts before the Lord, I knew that God was there in that upper room. It seemed to me that then God spoke to me quite clearly and directly, and what He said was this.

"Son, I give you a choice. You can be poor like these people all your days, but you will have Me; or you can become rich without Me. Which will you have?"

I sat for a long time as those people prayed. And then at last I answered, "Lord, let me be poor like these, so long as I have You."

The old saint ended his story very simply. "And I have indeed been poor all my days, but I have had God." And I knew that that gentle old man, whose spirit glowed with an inner radiancy, was great indeed in the sight of God.

I have related this experience in some detail because it illustrates several important elements in the life of prayer.
First, note the old man's telling phrase: "I felt a hunger for

prayer." Here was a person who in his late teens was already more than a novice in the practice of prayer. He knew its deeply satisfying communion and had grown to love it so much that at times it possessed him with aching longing. This is the thirst for God of which the Scriptures speak.

> As a hart longs
> for flowing streams
> So longs my soul
> for thee, O God.
> My soul thirsts for God.
> (Ps. 42:1−2 RSV)

This thirst for God is our response to the invitation of God. The initiative comes from Him. It is God who calls and we answer, at first with no very clear idea of what or whom we are seeking. It begins as a vague longing, but it goes on to become a purer desire for God Himself. Again the psalmist puts it plainly,

> When Thou saidst, Seek ye my face; my heart said unto thee,
> Thy face, LORD, will I seek (Ps. 27:8).

Charles Wesley repeats the psalmist's longing:

> Thou callest me to seek Thy face;
> 'This all I wish to seek;
> To attend the whispers of Thy grace,
> And hear Thee inward speak.

It was the whisper of grace that drew that young man to the prayer meeting and to his strange experience with God.

There is something starkly symbolic, too, in his response. He left the marketplace, with its clamor of buying and selling under its blaze of lights, and plunged into the black tunnel of the back street. The din behind him quickly faded as he groped his way uncertainly. He was by no means sure that the old chapel would be open at that late hour, but he pressed on until he saw the chink of light. Often after we have responded to this strange impulse to pray, we seem to be groping in the dark. Doubts assail, and it would be easy to turn back and rejoin the busy crowd. But if we press on, we find the Door.

The man sat in the upper room among the poor folk who had gathered to pray. As men reckon status, no one of any importance was there. They were a very humble lot, but they were the people of God and precious in His sight. The reality of their delight in God and their strong faith filled that upper room. With that reality before the young man, God put to him the great alternatives "Me and nothing else, or all things else without Me." Souls are deeply challenged in the atmosphere of burning prayer.

Do you think this harsh? Recall how Jesus spoke of gaining the whole world and losing one's soul, or how He put the love of God before all earthly loves. Think of the rich young ruler. This is not to say that wealth is evil. It can be. It can also be used gloriously as a stewardship under God. Each must discover God's will for himself. It is not that God wills to strip us of every earthly joy, but that if we are to enjoy Him, then every other love must come last, not first. When we are prepared to choose God for Himself, no matter what it costs, then He can really begin to fashion us according to His will.

Again Charles Wesley has a verse for it.

> I would be Thine, Thou know'st I would,
> And have Thee all my own;
> Thee, O my all; sufficient Good!
> I want, and Thee alone!

When we can say like that young man, "Nothing beside my God I want," we too will be far along on the path of prayer.

Beyond Time and Space

That pathway winds uphill all the way. Men of prayer often liken their quest for God to climbing a mountain. The wonderful vision that awaits us on the summit is the blissful hope that urges us up that celestial hill.

Beyond the bounds of time and space,
Look forward to that heavenly place,
The saints' secure abode:
On faith's strong eagle-pinions rise,
And force your passage to the skies,
And scale the mount of God.

"I will lift up mine eyes to the hills," those great, lonely heights over whose remote fastness an age-long silence broods. Far away they loom on the distant skyline, at once forbidding and inviting. Those who are weary of the noise and bustle of the market, the clamor of the mill, the strident din of the crowded streets, long for the utter stillness of the hidden glens and secret places. Those who are choked with the heat and dust of Vanity Fair long for the clean, cool winds that sweep over the massive flanks of the mountain that rises range after range to the crowning peak.

Puny man, so weak in himself, answers the call of the heights that beckon him to share their impregnable power—the "strength of the hills." And from the cloud that shrouds the summit issues the invitation, "Come up to Me into the mount and be there" (Exod. 24:12).

(We speak in parables. Symbols have to carry our thought where language fails.)

He who would reach the summit must enter the cloud. Suddenly the sunlight is blotted out, and the path disappears from view. Swirling mists—the most dreadful of all terrors to the mountaineer—close in, and a chilling coldness strikes to the very bones. Movement is reduced to crawling inch by inch. Fingers guide instead of eyes. The mountain that drew us threatens to become our tomb. When strength is gone, we can do nothing more than cling to the Rock. Then He comes, and joy begins to glow with golden incandescence; a strange warmth burns in the heart.

"And the appearance of the glory of the Lord was like devouring fire on the top of the mount" (Exod. 24:17).

For many of us, the entrance to the beatific vision—that is, to the sight of God—must be through this strange self-emptying that has sometimes been described as entering into the cloud. Indeed, one of the great mystical classics is called *The Cloud of Unknowing*. It is not everybody's way, but it does call attention to the fact that God is not perceived in the same way as objects and things are perceived. We feel God at deeper levels of being, and sometimes we have to unlearn before we can learn. We must let certain lifelong habits of thought go and surrender certain preconceived ideas. God is not at all like what we think or imagine. In some ways He is wholly and entirely other, utterly different, yet He is willing to make Himself known if we are prepared to receive Him as He is, to let God be God.

Prayer in its higher and intensive forms is the determined and arduous pursuit of fellowship with God. He who undertakes this quest must be resolved not to be deflected by any difficulty or temptation, but to devote himself entirely to the great Object of his growing love. He will encounter all manner of difficulties and hindrances; he will face manifold temptations and have as many adventures as Christian in *The Pilgrim's Progress*.

Beyond Fear

There is one recurring experience for which I would prepare the questing soul. There will be moments when the very reality of God's presence will fill us with dread and terror. We will feel the creature part of us shriveling before the awful majesty of the Creator. We will know God as a devouring, searing fire that burns and searches. We will begin to understand how heaven and earth must flee away from such a Being. A fear will possess us different from any other fear.

This fear is the basis of true worship. You will remember that strange phrase Scripture uses: "The God of Abraham, and the *fear* of Isaac" (Gen. 31:42; cf. 31:53). This fear is man's natural response to God's holiness and otherness. This basic experience prepares us for the recognition of the love of God. It redeems our worship from familiarity. It fills us with breathless awe and unspeakable reverence.

There are many such lonely battles to be fought, nights of wrestling with the strange Spirit that seizes us. Like Jacob we must endure to the end, refusing to surrender or disengage.

> With Thee all night I mean to stay
> And wrestle till the break of day.

One cannot describe the loneliness or the anguish of this encounter. It can be so severe as to become an agony. But if we persevere, He will bless us before He leaves us, for this is a period of testing and the reward is great.

> My prayer hath power with God; the grace
> Unspeakable I now receive;
> Through faith I see Thee face to face,
> I see Thee face to face, and live!
> In vain I have not wept and strove:
> Thy nature and Thy name is Love.

Wesley longed for that glorious moment of fulfillment. It remained the goal through all the long climb.

> Then let me on the mountaintop
> Behold Thy open face,
> Where faith in sight is swallowed up
> And prayer is endless praise.

Chapter 12

Mainly for Ministers

The person who prays is the prayer. He is both petitioner and petition. —Samuel Chadwick

For generations past, the enormous expectations of people concerning their pastors have been the subject of amused comment, and whole categories of virtues have been set out that we ought to possess: "The brain of Plato, the strength of Samson, the patience of Job, the skin of a rhinoceros . . ." The lists vary, but the point is the same. I always prefer the fun when laypeople bring it up. For a minister to say, "This is what you expect of me," and be half serious about it is by no means as funny, and he runs the risk of unconsciously stressing how far he is from the expectations. Yet it cannot be denied that our calling is burdened by an immense hope and ideal in the people's minds, and no man can expect to fulfill it all.

Nor do we improve the situation when we take on things we don't have to. I am sure it is part of our task to get laypeople to do everything they can and will do, so that we may be freer for our specifically ministerial tasks. It isn't always easy to get them to do it, I know, but if a minister develops the idea early in his ministry that he's "half an architect" or "a fund raiser" or "the organizer of rigmarole" or "an expert in printing" or this or that, it may easily misdirect his time. If we have an extra gift here or there, let's throw it in for good measure, but we are ministers of God—called, chosen, and (we hope) faithful, expecting ultimately to be judged by that, knowing that we cannot fail if (by grace) we had succeeded there.

Love and Prayer

I have been reading again the letters of Forbes Robinson. They inspired me when I was a candidate for the ministry, and they impress me still. What was the secret of his extraordinary spiritual power? Love and prayer. There is no question about it. Almost all who write of him comment on it.

I do not disparage scholarship, of course. But does anyone care now about his edition of *The Coptic Apocryphal Gospels* (despite the new attention directed toward these gospels by Oscar Cullmann)? More than half a century after his death at age thirty-seven, people still talk of his influence, and his letters still quicken the impulse to pray. Consider this advice: "You must at all costs have a quiet time. Give up work if need be. Your influence finally depends upon your own firsthand knowledge of the unseen world, and on your experience of prayer. Love and sympathy and tact and insight are born of prayer."

Love and prayer. There is the secret of powerful ministry. Can anyone analyze the link between them? Does God give us that supernatural love because (and as) we pray—and is prayer easier and more eager because we have the love? I'm not sure, but I'm thinking again on that point. Think with me.

The same idea emerges from a study of the life and work of the Anglo-Catholic Father Andrew. It is all love and prayer. It was quite fitting that an anthology of his writings was entitled *Love's Fulfilment.* How he loved people! And a minimum of three hours' prayer a day! When I read information like that, I just wonder whether these men had the same pastoral and preaching and organizing tasks piled on them as we have. How could they possibly get in three hours of prayer a day? Yet Father Andrew did—and shifted mountains of work as well. Love and prayer. We may be poor tools and know it, but perhaps it helps us to know where the tool needs sharpening.

It is great to know ministers who are encouraging their people in the practice of prayer. Should a minister be opposed to the prayer cell movement, it has little hope in his church; if his interest is only lukewarm, it has little more; if he is warmly encouraging, it can begin to spread at once; and if he takes the lead and says with conviction to his people, "I also believe in this; let us do it together," the most wonderful things can happen.

Pastoral Prayer

I once wrote about pastoral visitation and expressed the opinion that one of the distinguishing marks of a pastoral call (as distinct from a social call) is that a minister prays with his people. I stated that if a man is doing "speculative" visiting (that is, calling on people not from his congregation), it would probably embarrass them to offer to pray in their homes; but if it was a pastoral call in the strict sense of that word (a shepherd visiting members of the flock of Christ), he would offer to pray with them. To my surprise, this drew vehement resentment from a few ministers. They didn't simply disagree; they were angry. I could get no reasons—only plain and undisguised annoyance. It has remained in my mind as one of the minor mysteries of my career.

I recalled this incident sometime later when I received a letter from a man who has been very ill for three years. He had been compelled to retire at a comparatively early age with children still to educate. He knew his life was precarious, and making ends meet was a monthly miracle; but he was trusting in God, and I sensed a brave serenity in his writing.

Yet that isn't my point in telling his story. During the past three years that man had visits from twenty-one ministers in my denomination. Twenty-one! He had been in hospitals in different parts of the country, and his name and need had been passed on. He was very grateful for the pastoral attention he received.

But—here's the rub—out of those twenty-one ministers (some of whom visited him many times), only one ever prayed with him. Only one! On the brink of death for months, his mind burdened with thoughts of his wife and children, his own prayers stale and seeming to fall back on him, and his poor heart longing for some man of God to intercede for him to high heaven—and only one ever prayed with him!

I wrote to the man and tried to make some defense for my colleagues. I suggested that "although the visiting ministers had not prayed with him, doubtless they had prayed for him"—but it didn't satisfy my own mind and I doubt if it satisfied his.

This man was not being anti-clerical. He was amazed at the pastoral oversight he received, and he deeply loved the brotherhood. It was that one incomprehensible omission that he couldn't understand, and I couldn't understand it either. There are times of terrible testing when the most devout soul needs to have his longings spoken to God by someone at his side, and those of us who have that loving ministry can barely imagine the impoverishment of those to whom it is denied.

Dealing With Doubt

Consider another point. Ministers today, if they stop to think about it, are dismayed at the church's failure to win non-churchgoers. How do we reach the people outside the church, especially the doubters and agnostics? Ministers have made two main observations to me.

First, some say they have no real contact with agnostics at all and don't see how they can get it. Having pastoral charge of a half-dozen churches and every hour crammed with necessary duties, they have no time to assault unbelief in the way they would like and must leave this ministry to others.

We sincerely sympathize with this problem, but there is a clear response to it. Even if we have few direct contacts with agnostics, our people are making them every day. If we seldom hear the frank statement of doubt or unbelief, the people in the pew hear them often and, alas, don't always have the answers. Our course, then, is clear. We must give the people the right bullets to fire. We must instruct them so they will have more confidence in controversy. Some people have confessed that they are half-agnostic themselves, so we have two ministries in one: to give them the answers for themselves, and for their workmates. The specialized training of ministers will be fully employed here. To encourage the people—especially men—talk about their doubts will do good to us and still more good to them. John Wesley loved to appeal to men of "reason and religion"—both. We trust that we are still both and can make our people such also.

The second observation that ministers make regarding agnostics concerns the sincerity of the unbelief. "Isn't this talk of intellectual doubt a smoke screen for moral failure?" they ask. Their disposition is to brush the "doubts" aside and make a direct thrust at the "doubters'" sins.

That intellectual doubts are sometimes employed to evade a gnawing conscience is beyond question. Every minister with any length of pastoral experience has met many instances of it. But to move from this widely accepted fact to the assertion (or insinuation) that all expressed doubt is a self-generated coverup of dirtiness within is false, offensive, and even cruel. When I think of the lifelong sufferings some people have had to endure, I don't wonder that they doubt the love of God. Yet I know how much easier their burdens would be if they could believe. Hence this longing most of us share to carry conviction to their minds.

What is it worth to a man under great testing to be sure that

> . . . One above
> In perfect wisdom, perfect love
> Is working for the best?

It is beyond all price.

The agnostics include some of the kindest, most admirable people in the community. It is pure privilege to help them. It requires insight, delicacy, prayer, patience, and the frank admission that *we* haven't got all the answers either. All men are sinners, and some men fake doubts to stifle their conscience, but to assume that every agnostic is an immoral hypocrite is wrong.

The Word of Assurance

The distinctive characteristic of a minister per se is that he has a sure word about God. He can go to the pain-racked and nourish the faith in them that love is at the heart of all things. He can go to the dying and take the terror (though not the awe) from death. He can go to the bereaved and put comfort right in the core of their heart. He doesn't just "repeat the words." He is sure—and he can communicate something, at least, of his assurance to others. This is his special task. Some laypeople have it too, but the minister ought to have it above all.

If the minister is not eloquent or a "genius" with youth or a "superb" administrator, forgive him. He has a sure word about God. He's a minister! And if he hasn't a sure word about God, will it matter very much if he's all the other things? He fails at the very point he's appointed to meet; he's not a minister.

Where does that assurance come from? From God Himself of course. How does it come? Not in our college lectures, though much that is valuable comes that way. Not at our ordination, solemn and wonderful though that hour is meant to be. It comes from much private fellowship with God in prayer.

Never Off Duty

There is further reason why ministers should be masters of prayer: it is expected of them.

A judge remarked on a case, in which an ex-clergyman was involved, that it was a far greater sin for a priest to do wrong than for a layman. Why? Are they not both human and subject to the same temptations? Why should one be more culpable than the other? Dick Sheppard suggests in *The Human Parson* that the reason for this attitude is that laypeople think of pastors as a race apart, who by some magical ritual at ordination are removed from all the temptations of ordinary people. Consequently they expect ministers to be perfect and apply to them a far stricter moral code than they accept for themselves. That is why the sins of a minister will hit the headlines while the same offense by a layperson is scarcely news.

No matter how much we may protest and remind the world that we are recruited from the ranks of the laity, we must recognize there is a general awareness (in spite of the apostasy of our age) that Christianity claims to provide the finest possible type of manhood, and the world thinks it is entitled to see the evidence of that claim in its professional exponents.

If Christianity really works and is anything more than an ineffective idealism, it ought to be clearly demonstrated in the lives of those who can devote their whole lives to its study and who tell other people that they ought to live by its transforming power. It is precisely because of the tremendous claims of Christianity that ministers and their families—whether they like it or not—are watched more critically than any other people in our civilization. People who seem to have no interest in religion at all keep a sharp eye on the people in the manse. At home or on vacation, on bus or plane, in shop or street, every day and everywhere, the minister is never off duty. He is always on the job.

It is a sobering thought that for most people, the claim of Christ to be the Light and Savior of the world is either proved or disproved by what they see of Him in a minister. We are the key witnesses, either attracting men to Him or repelling them. In a real sense, what we say in the pulpit is of less importance than what we are.

The outsider, with every justification, expects to see a personality that patently demonstrates the truth of the sermons. How keen his observation is often escapes us, for it does not focus on the things that loom large in our minds, but on the little, unconscious traits of character that go to make up the real self. In the ceaseless examination to which the minister is subjected, it is the quality of the soul that counts, not his views on theology or churchmanship or politics. It is the way we speak as much as what we say, the warmth or coldness of our approach to the common man, our spontaneous asides rather than our set speeches, our willingness to help and our ability to mix that matter. The people outside the church and many inside are, in fact, assessing the quality of the minister's inner life. They want the evidence of that gracious and lovable spirit which they associate with the name of Jesus Christ.

There is only one way by which this spirit is acquired: the school of prayer. And so we pray:

Lord Jesus, give me a heart like Yours, as loving and patient, as kind, as tender, as faithful as Yours.

Let what I am drive no one from You, but rather let me draw men to Yourself. Amen.

Working on the Raw Material

It is fashionable in some quarters to assert that personality is really a matter of glands and the way in which the neural circuits of the brain operate. You will recognize this as the latest form of the materialistic argument.

There is an element of truth in it. Some people are naturally kind and will do anything for anybody; others are naturally moody, supersensitive, and irritable. Yet we praise the nice ones as if their goodness were a sign of grace, and we dislike and avoid the awkward ones as if their unattractiveness were due to deliberate ill-will. The fact is, we are not to blame for the raw material of our nature; we are responsible only for what we make of it.

It is easy to admire the brilliant and to be drawn to the sweet tempered, but their goodness may be little credit to them, since it is the result of a happily balanced heredity. It is fatally easy to be bored with the dull, to lose patience with the bad tempered, and to neglect the surly, the sharp, and the embittered, yet they may be in no way to blame for their temperament.

Unless a minister is on his guard, he may find himself regularly visiting those he likes and, without knowing it, postponing his calls on the unattractive. Our job is to assess the raw material of personality for what it is and to help people to make the best of it. We may find that the amiable, pleasant people whom everybody likes are actually making the least spiritual progress, while the difficult, miserable person is developing admirably. And while we are thus judging others, let us judge ourselves. Let us appraise our own gifts soberly and recognize our limitations, remembering that God, who knows the worst about us, has called us into His ministry because He has a job for us to do. We have to work on the raw material.

Some gifts every minister must have, and if they are absent or undeveloped we must earnestly ask God for them (James 1:5). People must find it easy to talk to us. If we are tense, cold, and unapproachable, we must ask the Holy Spirit to change our nature. If we are domineering, we must pray for the humility of Christ.

For many people, the only way to the Savior will be what they see of Him in us. So no matter what kind of personality we begin with, we must try to mold it into His likeness. Dick Sheppard writes again:

> It is beyond dispute the business of every [pastor] to transform his own life until all unconsciously it is capable of giving out the same kind of music that Jesus made in Galilee. . . . We are never abused or laughed at for being like Him. We are discounted because we are so unlike Him.

And so we pray:

> *O Master, the more we strive to follow You, the more we discover great traits of personality that still need to be redeemed. Stamp Your own image on our wayward, stubborn hearts, for Your name's sake. Amen.*

The Shepherd As Intercessor

A minister is the shepherd of his flock, the undershepherd of Christ. Part of that pastoral office is the responsibility before God for the growth and development of his people in the things of God. Much can be done by preaching and by teaching, but more can be done by prayer.

How do we intercede for people? Some ministers don't. It has never occurred to them that they have any obligation to do so. They pray, of course, for particular members in trouble, but not for each and every member regularly and consistently. Yet how much more effective their ministry would be if they did!

A pastor is a bridge builder between man and God, and the bridge is built by prayer. A minister is a priest, a true priest, when he makes himself the bridge by which the link is established. In the mystery of his intercession the connection is established through which divine power flows.

How then do we intercede for people? The membership roll, the Sunday school, the youth club, the women's organization, and the men's meeting all provide names for our prayer list. When a minister takes up a new charge and collects these lists, it seems a formidable roster. But there are 365 days in a year, so he does not panic. He prays for a few each day. Each day's visitation will enable him to attach significance to a name. The more regularly and systematically he visits, the sooner he will know his flock by name, as every good shepherd must.

There are two occasions when he will want to intercede. First, the day before he visits, when he is planning his round. He will pray that God will give him the insight to see the spiritual need, the wisdom to seek the helpful word. He will lift up that soul before God and pray that a new step in grace may be taken. Then after his visit he will again intercede in the light of his deeper knowledge.

Wonderful things happen when we pray for a congregation systematically. One minister told me how he was thus praying for some of his members when he came to the name of a man who was desperately ill. As he prayed, his hands began to move as if they were projecting some power. At first he thought he was deluding himself and stopped praying. Then he thought, "That cannot be right. Nothing must stop me from praying for my people." When he resumed praying, the hands again began their strange waving action. The next morning he called on this sick man and learned that a marvelous change had occurred in his condition at the very hour of that interceding prayer. That is exceptional, of course, but many ministers can tell of divine promptings that have come in such time of pleading for others.

Intercession should be full of thanksgiving for the access we have to the people and for what they are. We should thank God for the privilege of knowing them. "I cease not to give thanks to God for you," says the apostle Paul.

Visiting the Sick

Visiting the sick is specialized work for the minister. Some doctors now recognize that the minister has a part to play as important in its own way as medical treatment. But the minister has to know his job. To do it properly he needs instruction and practice. A blundering visit can do considerable harm. So let us consider a few general principles.

When people are ill they are usually supersensitive to sound. The noisy, cheery, loud-talking approach causes stress and tension in patients. They need quiet reassurance and encouragement. Most illnesses are depressing. Patients tend to worry and look on the black side. They need comforting. Find out what is worrying them and help by promising to do something for them. They may want a taped sermon or news about a loved one or some business concern. To tell them you will do this can lift great burdens and change their whole outlook.

When people become ill they have time to think. Often they begin to think about things they have been running away from for years. If they suspect they are seriously ill, they will be wondering about the real meaning of life and death and what is going to happen to them and to the loved ones they may leave behind. They need the comfort the gospel can give, the assurance that they are in God's hands, that all healing is of God, that death cannot separate them from God.

These truths can be presented without frightening them. They can be made to see that religion is precisely what they need at this time, and be persuaded to let their faith work. It is not easy to get this across in a crowded ward, and it can be embarrassing to kneel and pray as we would in a patient's home. But we can quietly take their hand and hold it while a prayer is softly spoken, which only they, ourselves, and God can hear. After such gentle ministrations it is not unusual for patients to settle down and have a restful sleep. The turning point of many an illness has been that blessed moment of prayer.

Even when health has not returned and patients have slipped away from us, prayer has lighted the last hours and enabled the pilgrims to feel the ground under their feet as they have crossed Jordan.

Blessings in Writing

Letter writing takes up a fair share of a minister's time. Much of it is routine: calling meetings, filling in returns, asking for information about a program. But much of it is, or could be, highly personal: a letter to a teenager starting the first job, to a student facing a final exam, to someone contemplating marriage, to a sick man, to a bereaved wife, to an anxious parent.

It is easy to be too busy to send such letters. In that case we are too busy. This kind of letter can become the treasure of the years, blessing not only the recipient, but many others.

Here is a little prayer one minister has used before he begins to write:

Lord Jesus, now I turn to correspondence. Let me recall that this also is Your work, not mine. Let me remember that I am addressing those who are very dear to You. Let Your Spirit breathe in my letters this day. Give me a kind heart, a clear mind, and a gracious pen. May I bring forth from the treasures You have given me things new and old. Teach me what to say and how to say it, that they may catch the echo of Your voice, for Your name's sake. Amen.

Some people have found great help in composing little prayers for various occasions and using their collection as a private book of meditations. Here, for example, is a prayer one minister uses for Sunday mornings:

Almighty God, today I must go forth to preach Your Word. Have mercy on me and touch these unclean lips with holy fire. You have called me to Your service, knowing me for what I am. I am not worthy to speak for You. You have forgiven me repeatedly; forgive again, Lord, so that I can go into that pulpit with a clean heart.

My preparation is not adequate. There is sin in the unfitness of my mind and soul. The neglect of the years condemns me. Had I listened more earnestly, thought more deeply, followed more faithfully, I should have heard Your voice more clearly. So take the poor offering I bring this day and use it as only You can.

Let me get out of the way, Lord, so that the people may see You, not me; hear You, not me.

Fill the house with heavenly power. Weave our adoration, praise, thanksgiving, prayer, and meditation into one great act of communion with You. Lift the burden from the heavy laden; open the eyes of some blinded one; enter some heart; and strengthen Your saints. Therefore, Father, speak now a gracious word through me to Your people. In Your pardoning grace behold Your servant and send me forth in Your name, for Jesus' sake. Amen.

Prayers like this compose themselves in a minister's mind as he brings all his ministry, act by act, into the presence of God. As he offers to God his day's work and sees its success and failure, he intercedes for his people, confesses his faults, and thanks God for the privilege of ministry. And since situations repeat themselves in a minister's work, his prayers will cover the same ground again and again. Whether he writes down the prayers or not, the phrases will be in his mind; so when he enters the sick room or kneels beside the kitchen table or prays with a man in his garden, his spontaneous prayer will be rich and adequate because it is prepared.

Such a man is his own prayer book. He will be known, though he himself knows it not, as a man of prayer. And those with whom he has prayed will know him for what he is—a man of God.